The Refusal of Politics

Incitements

Series editors: Peg Birmingham, DePaul University and Dimitris Vardoulakis, University of Western Sydney

An incitement is a thought that leads to a further thought or an action that solicits a response, while also testing the limits of what is acceptable or lawful. The books in this series, by prominent, world class scholars, will highlight the political import of philosophy, showing how concepts can be translated into political praxis, and how praxis is inextricably linked to thinking.

Editorial Advisory Board

Étienne Balibar, Andrew Benjamin, Jay M. Bernstein, Rosi Braidotti, Wendy Brown, Judith Butler, Adriana Cavarero, Howard Caygill, Rebecca Comay, Joan Copjec, Simon Critchley, Costas Douzinas, Peter Fenves, Christopher Fynsk, Moira Gatens, Gregg Lambert, Leonard Lawlor, Genevieve Lloyd, Catherine Malabou, James Martel, Christoph Menke, Warren Montag, Michael Naas, Antonio Negri, Kelly Oliver, Paul Patton, Anson Rabinbach, Gerhard Richter, Martin Saar, Miguel Vatter, Gianni Vattimo, Santiago Zabala

Available

Return Statements: The Return of Religion in Contemporary Philosophy
By Gregg Lambert

The Refusal of Politics
By Laurent Dubreuil, translated by Cory Browning

Plastic Sovereignties: Agamben and the Politics of Aesthetics
By Arne De Boever

From Violence to Speaking Out: Apocalypse and Expression in Foucault, Derrida and Deleuze
By Leonard Lawlor

Forthcoming

Agonistic Mourning: Political Dissidence and the Women in Black
By Athena Athanasiou

The Refusal of Politics

Laurent Dubreuil

Translation by Cory Browning

EDINBURGH
University Press

Edinburgh University Press is one of the leading university presses in the UK. We publish academic books and journals in our selected subject areas across the humanities and social sciences, combining cutting-edge scholarship with high editorial and production values to produce academic works of lasting importance. For more information visit our website: edinburghuniversitypress.com

© *Le Refus de la politique*, Laurent Dubreuil, Hermann Éditeurs, 2012
English translation © Cory Browning, 2016

Edinburgh University Press Ltd
The Tun - Holyrood Road, 12(2f) Jackson's Entry, Edinburgh EH8 8PJ

Typeset in Bembo
by R. J. Footring Ltd, Derby, UK

A CIP record for this book is available from the British Library

ISBN 978 1 4744 1674 0 (hardback)
ISBN 978 1 4744 1676 4 (webready PDF)
ISBN 978 1 4744 1675 7 (paperback)
ISBN 978 1 4744 1677 1 (epub)

The right of Laurent Dubreuil to be identified as the author of this work has been asserted in accordance with the Copyright, Designs and Patents Act 1988, and the Copyright and Related Rights Regulations 2003 (SI No. 2498).

Contents

Opening Opinion   1

[1] Apolitics and Politics   7

[2] Liveable Interruption   53

[3] Forms of Experience   75

Index   112

Opening Opinion

No. This *no* that is currently rising and rumbling on each and every stage of power is ancient; it is also new. Ancient in that every great political demand *contains* the possibility of larger objection, one that goes against the government *of* politics itself, and not just in this or that form, whether forged in elections, technocratism, accumulation of wealth, or force. New to the extent that numerous contemporary movements in Asia, Africa, Europe, the Americas are posing sharper questions about the risk of a return to order by their own hand. *Disdain for official politics*, widely shared throughout the world, is not in itself demobilisation. The *indignados* in the streets, peasants illegally cultivating land zoned for construction, protestors who *occupy* a putatively public space, in their vast refusal and their will to eschew disciplined organisation, they are all saying *no* to what lurks beneath political circumstance. But how difficult it is to see clearly the amplitude of this refusal! How impossible it might seem not to fall back into ordinary combat, to go beyond antipolitics without getting caught up in the more or less realist fantasy of an alternative *polis*!

In their successes and failures, these rebels remind us that our existences *in* the City do not mesh with the farce of political 'life', civic mindfulness or citizen conduct. Our engagement goes beyond cataloguing, voting and diatribes; we sense it in our professional relations, our loves, our travels, our desires. However, such an observation directly gives way to entertaining the idea that an 'other' politics (perhaps individual, informal or insurrectionary) could completely turn things around. But I am suggesting that if it is indeed urgent to rise up in disdain [*s'indigner*],[1] it is high time to refute the control of all by all, right down to the principles that justify the transcendent order of the City. We must hold the course and go so far as to *refuse politics*.

How's that? A desire to leave politics at the moment when the electronic winter of conformed global thought is taking hold, thought that dominates 3D inanity and whose internal pacification in the principal HQs rests on perpetual warmongering, impassioned populism and an informant mentality? Ah, I don't pretend that that doesn't leave things unchanged. I'm saying it isn't everything, that the hold of politics will not be eliminated by attacking only this or that programme, and that working outside programmability is all that remains. In that regard, the most harrowing problem is not abstention, nor vexation or exploitation: rather it is to *cling to the vain belief that all the ills of politics could have a political solution.*

The best politics strives to promote the collectivity's ability to *live well* [*bien vivre*], and it faces great difficulties in rising to this challenge. Let us help it then, contributing in our own way; let us denounce it if need be; let us not be dumbfounded by the rhetoric of divine right, the *fait accompli* or the laws of the system. *But above all, I want to live better.* According to the logic of their mandates, the forces of the City tend to reduce the scope of the real to their strict purview, all the more so given that their actions fail so blatantly. Ramparts were not built yesterday; however contemporary history is distinct in the construction of ever greater walls and in its sophisticated engineering. Today's planetary politics puts great stock and energy into concealing the outside of the *polis* as well as what the arts, feelings, thought, intensity, the inconstructible hold up in relief against capital Order and its insidious proclamations that all is given, neutral or done. The unbearable managerial discourse, the increased domination over the living, the permanent circus of elected representatives and managers, the gigantic enterprise of informative ideas, the destruction or systematic enslavement of certain animal groups – humans or others – should be met with revolt, uprisings, rebellions, revolutions. *But that is not enough.*

Desire for defiance permeates our times. Some of the recent anti-establishment movements are cause for concern in the official organisation of the world. Rather than working within a determined programme or making demands for a 'reassessment', these groups first target an essential institution of power: the tyrant during the Arab Spring; the centralising, planning state in France; continental China in Hong Kong; the economy of sports and the spectacular in Brazil; Wall Street or Washington in the United States; the European Bank in Greece. By calling it into question in this way – tacitly understood as 'radical' within the societies in question – these movements leave little room for the usual revolving door of politics, since the majority of eligible parties already participate in the system being denounced. That there is an effective absence of perspective on an 'organised revolution' only reinforces de facto the significance of this *no*, rather than rendering it vain, as the old Marxist or conservative interpretation doggedly insists. At the same time, these movements are galvanising new efforts at auto- or self-organisation, ranging from the creation of a parallel space of communication via the internet to the realisation of communes *in situ*. Such is the case of the '*zadistes*' in France, a sort of neo-indigenist movement that occupies and cultivates land that state or local authorities have just designated for the construction of an airport, a dam, a stadium and so on. Hope runs high: by metonymy, politics in its concrete form suffers a blow in that the totalising institution is challenged and further defied by attempts at collective existence that escape its grasp. Deception is proportional, but not unexpected. For example, how could we believe for an instant that a revolution channelled pre-emptively by electronic instruments of thought control (facebook, twitter and so on) could do more than modify a regime, simply redirecting its hold? How could we not see that a rhetoric of the majority ('we are the 99%') may utterly dissolve in the worst social order? How could we imagine liberating speech without recognising parlance, served pell-mell by a Beppe Grillo in Italy or a Dieudonné in France? How could we forget that utopian communities are not at all, by definition, free from authoritarianism and violence?

Above all, as long as political refusal (indeed anti-political affirmation) is not understood as more than itself, as long as circumstances of episodic rejection veil the virtuality of a *supplementary* opening toward a *non-political* elsewhere, even the liveliest and most thoughtful insurrections will fall short of their goals. One of the reasons behind this book is to help us understand what I am calling *apolitics*, this desire for an outside – liveable, intermittent – that neither condemns to indifference nor is doomed fatally to consolidate the empire. It is up to us to give voice to this *search for a liveable life that no politics could claim to build without destroying it immediately*, without dissolving it in the process of organising places and powers.

OPENING OPINION

This work was written as an introduction, at once elliptical and continuous. The first chapter of this book situates the refusal in relation to different contemporary theoretical attempts to renew politics, and makes the case for a greater rupture. The second moment takes up what is liveable in life by way of apolitical experience, in contrast to appropriations of the collective; logically, I touch on arts here as well. Finally, I draw up an incomplete inventory of means, forms of existence – often frail and fleeting – that make an exit toward *atopia* [*l'atopie*].

As a whole, the book draws on a parallel necessity to take into account political theories, the description of contemporary order in its concrete dimension, the ordinary or extraordinary life of every *I*, the accomplishments of the social-historical, the aims of politicians, the great rebellions at work in the world, the advent of a speech [*parole*], minor accounts and artistic works. Readers still curious may refer to two of my other works: *The Empire of Language*,[2] which specifically takes up political infiltration of everyday existence, and *À force d'amitié*,[3] which develops a more sustained attempt at an exit from closed space by way of impassioned friendship.

The title of this short preface, if it must be said, is a *palinode*,[4] following the example perhaps of the essay in its entirety, which joins in a long tradition of combined concern for *and* refusal of politics.[5]

Notes

1 See Stéphane Hessel, *Indignez-vous!*, English translation: *Time for Outrage!*, trans. Marion Duvert (New York: Twelve, 2011).
2 Originally published as *L'Empire du language: Colonies et francophonie* (Paris: Hermann, 2008). With corrections and additions as *Empire of Language:*

Toward a Critique of (Post)colonial Expression, trans. David Fieni (Ithaca, NY: Cornell University Press, 2012).
3   *À force d'amitié* (Paris: Hermann, 2009).
4   I am here taking up again a position on the *palinode* that I developed in an article of the same name in *Balthazar*, 3, 1998.
5   For a shorter and more 'hemmed in' version of the first half of this book, see my article in the issue of *diacritics* dedicated to *Negative Politics*: 'Negative Politics: At the City's Limit', *diacritics*, 39:2, 2009, pp. 5–20. Also for those fortunate enough to read Swedish, see 'Anteckningar om det Apolitiska', *Subaltern*, 2, 2010, pp. 26–31.

1

Apolitics and Politics[1]

[1]

As long as social discontent exists, the most immediate, the most *reasonable* solution is to change certain causes, certain effects, certain agents. In the most acute cases, the recommended therapy consists in a gigantic reorganisation of forces, a metabole of powers. 'The world is about to change its foundation', promises *The Internationale*, and, following the tradition begun by the Abbé Sieyès, the choir sings, 'we are nothing, let us be everything'.[2] However violent the alteration – and the last century has given us nearly everything, from the colonial yoke to its soft alternative, from banana dictatorship to the dictatorship of the bureaucratic proletariat, from change in continuity to fully policed societies – the *foundation* of the foundation remains the same, rarely questioned. That is to say: all metamorphosis remains squarely on the plane of politics; only the way we define this plane varies, ranging from popular government and representation to the insurrectionary battle, from the nation, race to lifestyles and on to revolution.

In any case and despite immense divergences and incompatibilities, one point remains constant: discontent, unrest and refusal continue to be channelled by political action, whether administrative, bloody, molecular, spectacular or other. The idea thus emerges that beyond, beside or outside political demands, anguish and rejection, we can also (or perhaps *rather*) make out a desire for greater defection, a break not only with the police and the grand farce of power, but more broadly with politics, the political and policies.[3]

[2]

Obviously, in general we are programmed in such a way that this consequence, and the doubt associated with it, appears absurd. Programmed by what, I could only here give a brief and allusive list. Programmed by our biological constitution, which makes us into social animals with a penchant for conformism and whose conflicts, interests or faults work themselves out 'naturally' within an *organised* collective body. Programmed as well by social prescription in all its diffuse points, which is, precisely, the virtue of such a prescription. Programmed by our formative institutions, among whose ranks figure schooling and the media (functioning as an intellectual conduit). By the expansion of the sphere of politics, under the combined effects of a race to make reparations in the recesses of existence and an intensification of the becoming world of the world [*devenir monde du monde*]. Constantly programmed thus, by these manoeuvres and a thousand others, and without taking into account the foresight involved in the fact that there is a palpable interest in not dreaming of such a brutal rupture as soon as we are even slightly *integrated*, we tend not to allow ourselves to go so far as to reject politics. At the same time, we make vague gestures in this direction every day or nearly so, without admitting it to ourselves. We find figures, harbingers even, of an impossible exit that we both recognise and dread. Beyond the enchanting perspectives, the usual deceptions, the perpetual wrongs and disagreements, is not the decisive problem of politics politics itself? And what would allow us to think the postulates, the forms, the repercussions of such an acquittal of politics, discharging it from all duties and debts?

[3]

This apolitical refusal can hardly speak its name in philosophy today. What prevails in such a discourse [*parole*] will be the multiplication of theoretical instances allowing us to censure – sometimes even violently or 'radically' – a portion of it, one side, one conception of politics, in order to get at another manner or another space to cultivate, to preserve. Thus the hope in biopower as a means to ward off biopolitics (as in Giorgio Agamben or Roberto Esposito),[4] politics to counter the police (Jacques Rancière),[5] the multitude against the State (Michael Hardt and Toni Negri),[6] the 'to-come' [*à-venir*] facing off with all *Realpolitik* (in the texts of Jacques Derrida or Chantal Mouffe),[7] the community of the political against communal politics (Jean-Luc Nancy),[8] the practice of intrapolitics against imperial politics (Alberto Moreiras),[9] minimalist versus maximal politics (Jean-Claude Milner), the list could go on.[10]

These articulations, at times taken in true binary opposition, at other times drawn out of the time of a differance, have their virtues. Thus, the recent insistence on the biopolitical has helped us grasp more fully the amplitude of politics' hold over 'life' – and it seems, on closer examination, that the reign over *bios* and *zōē* is a temptation as old as politics, only now taking on new arms. Similarly, there is little doubt that the figure of the multitude has jammed the old political machine, even though the cogs have quickly been set back in motion. In the same way, the relation between the *polis* and *police* has indicated the type of dictatorship that is striving to establish itself as a global model. Despite its messianic undertone, the distance of the future 'to come' has encouraged us never to believe in the consistent unity of *one* political time or action. And, at the very least, the fact that something political [*du politique*] – I would not say the *concept* of the political – orients our existences without being fully enmeshed within instituted politics may account for the easily felt discord and may help to situate the dream of doing politics outside any system.

However, how difficult it is for me not to see in these *articulations*, and many others, a repeated and tireless effort at conceptual conservation: 'we must protect the concept of the Political'. On the other hand, we must ask if capital Politics is capable of resolving in full all the afflictions of *politics*. From there, we should then ask: if the wrong is not to be resolved politically, is it still worthwhile to conserve the claims of a well-worn category? Despite the mixed contributions of an 'articulated' analysis of politics, must we really stop in our tracks, and make a mystical return to a *noble action* or *grand conception*, one that had apparently become tainted, obscured, deformed, tarnished by the dirty work of the police, the partisan, the ruler and the present? Nothing guarantees that ways to think politics and to act politically would be radically different when they're 'good' or 'best practices'. And, if relations of intensity exist, then everything that enters politics reproduces, to varying degrees, the wrong that is attributed to the police, biopolitics and to every negative presentation taking part in it. These gradations are not negligible; they condition the effects of domination and the types of liberation possible. It is because of them that not all regimes are equal and that their differences are perceived through individual and group experiences. On the other hand, the levels of intensity bring us back to their source, one that is bound within a collective postulation of a *totalising organisation of life*, alias politics, understood within the vague precision of its semantic extension.

Since the slightest separation of degree has an effect on the fact that I eat, speak, love and create, an absolute indifference to *all* politics – apoliticism, if you will – is a strange attitude, one held by the all too powerful and those completely deprived of power – for whom, at bottom, change is no longer possible. Who then can assure that this renunciation will ever be complete? Nonetheless, beyond the problems and solutions of practice, associations or regimes, every political breakdown produces and reinforces the intuition of the inevitable. Defections from politics will only ever be met with partial refashioning – sometimes indispensable, sometimes accessory. They make visible, by every breach, the possibility of something other than politics, something that would not simply precede politics. It is not a question of promoting *apolitics* as the direct and automatic remedy for the ills of politics (a consolation is not a cure), nor of discerning an alternative or anarchist mode of government. What is at stake is rather the intellectual apprehension of a-political productions, and the preliminary examination of what they can offer us.

[4]

In the last two or three decades, the doctrines of *political articulation* have accumulated a gigantic body of 'omnidirectional' critical texts as well as countless obstacles in order to fight against the legitimacy of any exit from the grand fortress of politics. There is really nothing more ordinary than this in philosophical tradition, except that the particularity of contemporary philosophy is to transform the *others* of politics into *other ways of articulating politics* [*transformer les* autres *de la politique en d'*autres politiques]. As a frontline maverick, Alain Badiou has, for his part, attempted to save politics without recourse to articulation, refuting both *the political* and the distinction with the *police*. This effort responds to any and all conceptual diffraction by massively reasserting *politics*. This position is established however only at the expense of rolling out cumbersome phenomena and philosophemes. For Badiou, not only is politics not tied to the State, it also becomes independent of history, favouring instead a mystique of the event. It is a very practical thesis, one that intends to shield itself from any attempt to judge politics according to its implementation or execution. Furthermore, biopolitics, the political and the police are for him but fictions to be dissipated; such a multiplication of categories carries no meaning, no truth for him. In one of his chapter titles, Badiou implies that Rancière, because he 'does not do politics' (in Badiou's sense of the term), engages only in 'apolitics'.[11] Strangely, Rancière therefore finds himself on the side of the State, which is itself 'a-political',[12] since it too does not correspond to Badiou's definition (*QED*).

We quickly see then the great contrast to what I am attempting here. First of all, the theoretical focus on *politics* (in which I partake) is not for me the occasion to *exclude* heterogeneous conceptions from the party line nor to *purge* a concept.[13] Rather, this focus allows us to complicate how we understand our experience. The gesture that consists in separating the wheat from the chaff, distilling *Politics* in all its fullness from its shadow others, seems to me more regressive than fundamentally innovative in relation to the strategies of articulation. What is then missed yet again is the possibility of an apolitics that would not be pronounced in the name of politics. In the meantime, however, one hauls back in ideas of '*pre*-political'[14] entities, themselves just as traditional. Finally, the ability of this rare and event-driven politics to make itself into a 'politics of non-domination'[15] may leave us puzzled as long as the conceptual armoury of philosophical authority is held in place, without question and without critical distance. The ponderous difficulty for Badiou to *think* contradiction and through contradiction may leave us fearful that he remains a prisoner to principles that reduce, in advance and in spite of everything, politics to a schematic debate in which one must outwit all adversaries. In fact, even when the desire to work for *a* 'politics of non-domination' begins to make itself heard, a discourse arises bloated with 'the law of the concept'[16] or 'I impose' and 'I forbid',[17] all redolent of the stale rank and file command of the concept.

[5]

The theoretical articulation or restoration of politics therefore bluntly refuses apolitics as inadmissible. Contemporary philosophy is far from being the unique bearer of radical doubt concerning an *exit*. It would be worthwhile to go back over the epistemic victory of the twentieth century that certifies, by way of the *social sciences*, that politics is at least the ineradicable dimension of our lives, and at worst 'our' sphere in its entirety. To recognise the *possible* political formatting at every moment has become a tireless and urgent task. This does not however imply in any way that we all adhere to the nearly ubiquitous consequence that *all* life remains within the limits of the *polis*. The attention that the social sciences and critical analysis have brought to the construction of modes of human existence encourages us to understand politics well beyond its conventional centres of practice (sect, corporation, party, state, nation, union and so on). Such attention does not however demonstrate that there is total politicisation without remainder.

[6]

The apolitical I'm elaborating is then the incident of an incidence [*l'incident d'une incidence*], the defection from common organisation that gives rise to the proposition of an exteriority that is impossible *de jure*. In the search for a break that would not simply be *re-integrated*, we need a more precise characterisation of politics. I see it as the empirical summation of heterogeneous practices that establish the collective order. The social would then begin every time the collective is regulated; or, at least, the inchoate social takes form when, in an animal group, prerogatives of rank and rules of distribution are established (the dividing of provisions, roles and so on). The social would be likely to emerge in a contingent setting with *more than one* [*à plus d'un*]. Society would *delimit* an orderly collective, one committed to its own perpetuation beyond that of its present members. It would constitute a generalisable space for every order of the social and every social order. Politics would be the gesture that establishes the order itself, or what organises the organisations. In response to the questions *why this society rather than another?*, or even *why society at all?*, one is simply told *because there is politics* [*parce que politique il y a*].

The distinction between *the political* [*le politique*] and *politics* [*la politique*] can be put forward for contrary reasons: one chooses *the political* in order to mark neutrality, which would be the absolute principle, in the German-Greek tradition – or in order to indicate a stratification of political action, one not instituted, outside of parties and voluntarily molecular. In any case, *social*, *society* and *politics/the political* form an interwoven, normative system in which each loops back to the other. The social, which is formed ad hoc, can legitimise society taken as a collective, which in turn legitimises *politics/the political* [*de la (ou du) politique*], thus closing the circuit. This is because politics is its own end, drawing its own limits [*s'arrête à soi-même*]. To say in turn that it depends on the gods, nature or history remains both a strong and a weak argument. *Strong* to the extent that it establishes the fiction of the founding of the City that is in sum immutable, inhuman, exterior and at the same time *intended* for the interior. Weak, since no one truly believes it. If a complete separation between politics and its authority exists, then, in the meantime and for *current affairs*, everything comes back to the *polis* (by means, if necessary, of speeches interspersed with references to Athena or the Lwa in Vodou). If not, by constantly appealing to the will of Allah, signs, oracles or the lessons of *history*, we are de facto politicising these non-political fictions. One grows weary of everything, even reading the future in tortoise shells. And, in these different cases, theoretically and practically, politics strives to justify and to close politics.

Power, domination are means to hold the order together and often develop, for the agents involved, into ends in themselves. They are at play at the most rudimentary levels of social prescription in the forms of conformism, habitus, *parlance* [*parlure*],[18] politeness, and in the prohibition which we are first initiated into as children (*don't do that*). Politics, designating the responsibility of ordering, is at least latent every time this *necessity* for social organisation is expressed, and overt in specific instances such as in rights (I'm not speaking of justice), the State, the nation and so on. I am developing, let us say then, an extremely pessimistic outlook, one that I take ironic pleasure in finding to be rather widespread (although without any of the conclusions that I am drawing) among the apostles of the bounty of the City, as, for example, when John Rawls observes in passing that 'political power is always a coercive power'.[19] As concerns the conceptions of politics without order, as we have just seen, it still remains to be proven that they accomplish this suspension in their diction, or that they do not reintroduce order. These figurations of politics drained of everything that makes it into an insistent experience partake in the recovery of apolitics, which I will develop more fully below. They are among the most desperate attempts to re-establish a *faith* in politics. The 'concept' – which is never whole and unitary in discursive thought – can neither orient nor contain politics. The influence of the social-historical is a decisive factor here. According to this experience, notably in its human form, politics proves capable of inhabiting everything without being everything. It is also shot through with discontent and discord, which can be partially reduced. Oppression and neutralisation, including recourse to brute force as the cradle of communicative action, are powerful means, perfectly capable of keeping in check or reducing to silence countless adversaries.

The result is not, however, complete, even in the most extreme cases of oppression and destruction (such as the Nazis or the Khmer Rouge), and politics is not identical to the consensus.[20] Apolitics is based on the persistence of discord, but it is born with the supposition that over and above all arrangements with political order – or with the heterogeneity of politics as order – a persistent inaptitude lingers, which must be swept away.

[7]

Politics is manoeuvred, developed on a small scale. Without the participation of individuals in the great game, the battle would be over before the first shot. According to the *Analects*, Confucius laid out two planes of power, one of administration and rights and the other of virtues and rituals. As a result, respecting filial and fraternal piety is, he said, equivalent to direct participation in government.[21] In more contemporary terms, let us take note of *macro-* and *micro-*politics, the link between the molecular and the molar, or between the diffuse and the concentrated.[22] These terms have to be perceived as resources for critique and rejection.

Among the forms of everyday *resistance* (theft, disguise)[23] one finds a mass of struggles simultaneously localised and converging against a legal and diffuse domination. Micropolitics sometimes acts as preparation for a movement on the molar level (food riots that precipitate revolutionary action), or as individual reparation for a wrong otherwise impossible to redress (poaching as a means to counter systems of exclusivity). Structurally, this rebellion supports secret or banned societies within societies (the Ku Klux Klan, the mafia, the Yakuza). Silently, it further displaces the goals and alibis of the majority, such as, for example, in antisocial sexual practices or not voting. Such actions multiply and are not satisfied with *representing* the political apparatus on another level. This is precisely their point. They have their limits – using the flag as a rag does not put an end to the nation, although the sacred status and the 'natural cohesion of the country' does veer towards the ridiculous. Nonetheless, they demonstrate a very real effectiveness that often absorbs the virtual excess of the negative.

Apolitics cannot be instituted, and, generally, its manifestation on the macroscopic level is so canalised by political action that we scarcely see it there. On the molecular level, which is more often its milieu, it cannot be systematically identified with every act of resistance or contravention, however much they may lay claim to politics in effect. Powers are so structured that even everyday utterances are ordered and arranged in advance. Such structuring is put into place collectively and is propagated by way of general prattle, books, schools, the media, sciences or laws – all *ways of speaking* that are sensitive in tone, voice, syntax, inflection, rhetoric, jargon and patterns. Frantz Fanon keenly observed this in colonialism as early as the 1950s.[24] Following a few decades after him, I have further argued that the *simple* fact of speaking (or remaining silent) can enter into a phraseology that takes the place of thought, making speakers the messengers of the established order, whatever their *intentions* might be.[25] Speech [*parole*] that breaks the installation of parlance [*parlure*] is carried by a molecular refusal that goes against institutional as well as trans-individual planes of imperial reality. Most often, this already unheard effort *to speak* coalesces around a minority movement of politicisation – unless, on the other hand, it makes way for a secondary parlance, alas also in use. The American feminist movement sums up the micro-functioning of domination with the slogan: 'the personal is the political'. We are thus called on to recognise the multiplicity of masculine domination, which cannot be reduced to the sexual stratification taking place in the headquarters of meta-European corporations. *Alas*, the soundness of the argument is quickly accompanied by a step backwards, which, aimed at the *personal*, strives violently to deny the possibility of non-politics. The article by Carol Hanisch that popularised the formula in 1969 ends, as if by coincidence, in praise of '"apolitical" women' (those outside militant activism) who are in fact 'very political ...'.[26]

[8]

After decades and centuries of activism on the fronts of sexual difference and race, it may seem that acute concern for the diffuse goes hand in hand with neglect of the concentrated; at least we often read and hear this kind of remark. When the debate is configured by a clear division between the micro and the macro, when the two levels coincide only by chance, we are dealing with a strategy as stupid as it is effective. Insisting on *identity* or the *subject*, as has become standard, does not guarantee that we remain within the diffuse. Thus, identity politics has responded to a concentrated *and* pulverised situation in molecular reactions; its distillation into a slogan or rallying cry for action in American corporations and elections clearly demonstrates its densification. The apparently non-partisan aspect still cherished by certain identity militants (feminine, gay, queer and so on) corresponds to the inferior degrees of concentration, which delay mass treatment and short-circuit diffusion, more prompt to escape the order of the City. – Inversely, *indigenismo*, for example, is far from figuring the radical alteration that seems to give hope to numerous combatants in Latin America.[27] That (post)colonial censorship of the indigenous did indeed occur, there is no doubt. As for the governmental resurrection of a sort of 'indigenous sentiment of life', to twist [*détourner*] Suzanne Césaire's expression, I am highly sceptical.[28] A former, diffuse form of control, a remnant from civilisation before the Native American genocide, and intellectually *reconstituted*, becomes the paradigm of a concentrated politics to reinvent. We begin to speak of an *indigenous* mode of production, *indigenous* social norms, *indigenous* methodology, all of which needs only to spread across the country. The content, the definition of the indigenous – like that of the Negro, women and so on – risks moving in the direction of a naturalised self-evident identity, thus leaving in place the political frames that assign this identity. Self-proclaimed queer thought that strives not to lapse into this same situation is, in the end, only capable of proposing (in the words of Judith Butler) a 'new configuration of politics', since 'the deconstruction of identity is not the deconstruction of politics' (we can all breathe easy now, I was getting worried). The ethical as a supplement arrives just at the right time to give the impression that something has, however, happened. In this way, we go from one book to another, from *Gender Trouble* to *Giving an Account of Oneself*.[29] Concern for the diffuse has managed in the end to shrink the political down to the subject, instead of seeing the signs of an even greater fracture.

[9]

The totalitarian tendency of politics comes from the same drive, raised to molecular and molar levels, towards complete lockdown. A totality is designated, set as a goal to achieve, which immediately takes control of the diffuse and the concentrated alike. The totalitarian proliferation of politics is a declaration ('*totum sum*'), one achieved by saturating all possibilities. Extending the playing field and imposing general uniformity are methods that Stalinism, Maoism and Nazism have all adopted enthusiastically. The technological, spectacular and standardised consumer dictatorship that is being exported under the rubric of liberal democracy is yet another undertaking of political totalisation. Here the individuality of the actor – although undermined from all sides – remains a shimmering safe haven that allows for some movement since any effect from public speech or gesture has been partially and pre-emptively neutralised. When Giovanni Gentile developed a theory of the *Totalitarian State* (as he christened it), he envisioned a political ascendancy over the real that would not in any way remain at the level of statism – fascism as a 'total conception of life'.[30] What the 'totalitarian' experience of social history furnishes is a name to a claim that is of the same essence as politics, but one that more or less takes rigid form.

It has become commonplace to challenge the idea of totalitarianism by associating it systematically with its phraseological use during the Cold War. If this usage has been established beyond doubt, then it is certainly expedient to find in it a pretext to ban a word. Gentile and Jünger, who began analysing the totalitarian postulation in the 1930s or 1940s, were already looking at more than just fascism or sovietism. Gentile declared objectives that in the end did not coincide with Mussolini's regime, and Jünger announced 'total mobilization' as the condition of the era 'in general'.[31] The Frankfurt School followed with a critique of totalitarianism that included many other regimes besides just those of the Eastern Block;[32] even Simone Weil, in 1943, spoke of the 'totalitarian, police-ridden' monarchy of seventeenth-century France.[33] Against a jittery reaction – shot through with paralysing, historicising scruples and apologetic tendencies that would absolve communism of any non-fortuitous resemblance to current or past characters and deeds – I maintain the utility of the category of totalitarianism.[34] Even beyond the historical example, we quickly see that the all of politics [*'la' politique*] aims to take a maximum hold on the all of life [*'la' vie*]. We are thus no longer dealing with a battle between two conceptions of society ('open' or 'closed', as Popper has it[35]), but with the differential instalment of a total programme.

[10]

Apolitics would be a *deictic refusal* that allows for the *affirmation of an irreducible outside*. In its elementary form, a rejection of what currently exists puts on display the incoherency, worthlessness and peril of any political *thing*. Gradually, the entire conventional association that makes up a *polis* is threatened by the deictic refusal of a place, a situation, an authority. Furthermore, social prescription, which defends organisation (the very stuff of politics), incites us to circumscribe denunciation, even to rebrand it as claims made by certain sectors. We should consider the social revolution as the supreme example of co-opting the refusal for the sake of political necessity. Of course, we have absolutely nothing to substitute, to put in *the place* of politics, which would lead to both the logical problem of renovating our categories and the empirical tendency to return to order by default. The political interruption in the refusal makes way for the temporary appearance of an exterior that would not be of any *polis*. When the former slave Epictetus redefined the limits of liberty for those who rule socially; when, centuries later, following this example, Julien Coupat,[36] accused in all but name, wrote from his cell to *Le Monde* that 'society today [...] is in effect a failed prison';[37] there and in every similar situation, or politic order, in its preferred definitions, wavers. But, most of the time, these instances of rupture are then merged into a particular programme that restores the usage of politics (government of the self and/or disdain for the *res publica* in Stoicism, from Marcus Aurelius to late Foucault; for Coupat, insurrectionary rhetoric). The *affirmation of an outside* is thus crucial, that which fractures the superb, omnipotent domination of politics.

[11]

Exaggerating a bit, we could say that I have reproduced offstage what Rancière put forth in *Disagreement* as a politics that, valorising dissensus and the incommensurable, would be 'always local and occasional'.[38] Oddly, then, that would make Badiou right in his assessment of apolitics. Rancière's goal, by way of articulation, is to keep the interruption *within* the political domain. This, to my mind, means containing the danger theoretically, while at the same time harnessing its force in practice, in the service of a politics of uprising, punctuated by protest slogans (those of October 1961,[39] May 1968). These episodes of equality thus serve as a form of 'recollecting of an event that constituted the inscription of the presupposition of equality'.[40] By arguing that 'the political community is a community of interruptions, fractures ...',[41] Rancière immediately reclaims and re-situates the refusal, thereby denying the possibility of an outside. Once euphoria and equality have been consummated, a trace will remain in the form of 'words of equality [*phrase égalitaire*]',[42] half-erased on the monument commemorating those who died making democracy a reality, erected in the very *centre* of the police state. 'Passers-by, remember ...'[43] – I do not deny that a certain politics *profits* from these hiatuses and that, in the end, every relaunching develops out of dissatisfaction [*mécontentement*], which is not always disagreement [*mésentente*]. On the other hand, in stopping at interruption, then reinscribing it immediately into politics by making it part of the very functioning of politics, Rancière both uncovers and eschews the apolitical.

I could give a comparable description of Laclau and Mouffe's project. They recognise political limitations and insist on 'dislocation' ... but then proceed to relocate it delicately within the framework of 'radical democracy'.[44] Derrida refers to an 'incommensurable friendship' that would unhinge the gates of the *polis*, and this friendship is constantly put off in the service of a politics of *philia* – if not unavoidable at least unavoided.[45] In short, it is not surprising that the greatest contemporary thinkers on politics are already describing apolitics, sometimes with great precision. And it is expected that these descriptions go unnamed, that they struggle to reconstruct or minimise the incident in favour of a *political* discord – that will only exist in remaking the faulty ordering of order [*ordonnancement*].

[12]

In order to better understand the possibilities of refusal, I am going to formulate and examine in more detail three concurrent hypotheses: the non-political exists; politics itself is not absolutely politicised; which, in turn, creates the condition for a refusal of politics.

In approaching apolitics, we first have to recognise the existence of a non-political – which would not, however, pre-emptively lump all instances of it together in advance. It is a delicate task. As we've seen: with contemporary advocates of a discontinuity to politics, the exterior is always more or less *determined* by the interior. For its part, theoretical pan-politicism confirms, willingly or not, differences of intensity or application, making politics into a total but not integral dimension. Mouffe confines politics to a *becoming*, and, just as abruptly, claims that it 'determines our very ontological condition'.[46] In perfectly emblematic fashion, Slavoj Žižek speaks of the 'hidden *political* process that sustains all these "non-" or "pre-political" relationships' and argues that 'in human society, the political is the englobing structuring principle, so that every neutralisation of some partial content as "non-political" is a political gesture *par excellence*'.[47] Taking a synthetic position, Jean-Luc Nancy writes that politics is distinct from 'spheres that are, strictly speaking, foreign to it [...]: the ones labelled more or less correctly *art*, *thought*, *love*, *desire*, and all the other possible ways of designating rapport with the infinite', before culminating in a hierarchical codicil – 'to think the manner in which these spheres are heterogeneous to the properly political sphere is a *political* necessity'.[48] In all these examples, the non-political is at best accepted only through its *Aufhebung* in the *polis*, a step on the way to the analysis of the event or its becoming. If the non-political exists, its verbal designation already makes it dependent on the order that, in fact, strives for totality. The minority makes itself heard from the majority. If it is a question of thinking *with* words, we mustn't give in to the *political* temptation to see the non-political as a simple state, reducible to its positive conversion. Without a doubt the conceptual propensity to contain the non-political serves a purpose: it responds, at the reflexive level, to the totalitarian postulation of powers. It reminds us that politics works to control the non-political. This control justifies states of exception, bodies and places in the margins and on the peripheries, tolerance for supernumerary groups whose institutionalisation, while ratifying a sort of exteriority, aims at surreptitiously politicising the contents by way of the very principle of institution. Designation of a non-political is unstable and wavering; it can include the refraction of an established order looking to absorb its negative double. However, *total* success at control has yet to be achieved.

Although phenomenology may have abused the formula to such an extent that I hesitate to take it back up, *there is* [*il y a*] seems an adequate expression in this case. There is the non-political [*il y a du non-politique*], and its discursive delimitation runs the risk of determining it incorrectly. For example, there is the non-political in scientific statements. Putting Lysenko and the dream of Soviet genetics side by side cannot justify the theoretical depoliticisation of all science. Objects, conventions, reasoning, experimental protocol in the sciences are politically charged. Despite its organised human form, science may nonetheless *point to* [*fait signe*] a non-political real that coheres to the 'inconstructible'.[49] The theory of evolution can be dated to Darwin's time, and it profoundly bears the imprint of contemporary debates over power and persistence. Nonetheless, its heuristic method calls attention to a non-political part of the world, where the adaptation of a genetic trait is structurally without a link to the *polis*. That my brain functions by neuron connections is non-political despite the fact that the parameters of my growth and survival are inscribed within the *res publica* or that descriptive models of cognition can borrow from metaphors that 'naturalise' the capitalist enterprise (with conscience as a *global work space*, and so on). The same could be said of the constitution of the 'I', through its thoughts, words, feelings, action. Nothing establishes that everything there is political, even though each element could become so *to a certain degree*. The equations between plurality, collectivity, group and society are not sufficient. To advance the hypothesis of a real *without* a link to politics, in its diffuse or concentrated states, amounts to positioning politicisation as a powerful though adventitious and non-determining phenomenon. Politics is not the sphere of spheres, nor is it the all-encompassing principle, nor the advent of *Aufhebung*: it is a regime, both totalising and interrupted.[50]

[13]

Let us conjecture that in spite of the ascendancy of intellectual powers and *certitudes*, no politics establishes itself absolutely as long as non-politics emerges, which also excludes the image of a domain reserved specifically for it. An immediate corollary follows concerning the inability of politics to politicise itself through and through. The subject is well known, though it is often glossed over: the why of politics is not political. Several explanations, more or less compatible, can be put forward, and

I will cite a few for the record before spending more time on the consequences of the hypothesis. Aristotle's position, which situates the political animality of man in *nature*, thereby suspends the possibility that a totalising postulation could be carried out absolutely.[51] A metaphysical disposition on the lack of the real would likewise provide evidence for incompleteness, as can be seen in a certain pessimism of finitude. A logical hurdle limits politics' ability to be political completely and thoroughly, right down to its *quod*.[52] The ordinary category of politicisation, whether transhistorical or not, enters into this debate. The fiction of an *exit* from the state of nature hinders by definition the founding contract from being political without remainder, since its conditions of creation, its *impetus* is situated in the non-political. What Castoriadis called 'the imaginary institution of society' refers back to the inside–outside that constituted, collective bodies invent as their origin. And finally, empirically, at the subjective level, even when we know and explore the ramifications of diffuse politics, a mixed impression lingers that everything is affected even though it is not. At the collective level, the smallest experience in militancy may be enough to make one think that politics, in its many actualisations, is never full, and that its *self-evidence* is void [*son évidence est vide*].

That the existence of politics is non-political evidently modifies the determining relation of the negative that is most often adopted today. Simply inverting the relation would be deceptive. We would do better to note the extent to which the fragility of non-politics (all too often used to dismiss it) corresponds to the profound *shortcoming* of politics. Broken promises, lies, manipulation, indoctrination, shows of force, flip-flopping, hypocrisy all add to the pre-existing fact that politics falls short of itself [*se fait à soi-même défaut*]. To make up for this lack, a

THE REFUSAL OF POLITICS

every standardisation, every computer function, every *enhancement* follows from human decisions that are both micro- and macro-political. Consequently, the computational hypothesis in cognitive sciences, which elucidates the neuronal by way of artificial intelligence, serves largely to present digitalisation as *natural* and *inexorable*, including any inconstructible portion. The equation of politics with technique does not however constitute [a] reduction of one to the other, as a reactionary interpretation might suppose (even if it would have the great merit of [an] all too rare denunciation). It is an opportunist strategy that [at]tempts to give a specific form to totality under the guise of an [in]disputable universal. Techno-logy – it is indeed a question of [a] discursive act, or, more accurately, of a *phrase* – is a measure of [the] expansion of politics, spurred by the necessity of mastering [ev]olutions and the growth of applied knowledge. Union-[iz]ed, partisan or state bureaucracy, so maligned by Trotskyism [and] other movements, is a form of techno-political control. [Bur]nham and Rizzi, if their writings do not live up to their [...] intuition, had the merit of recognising in the 1930s and [194]0s the convergences of managing practices in Soviet-style [plan]ning, Nazi hierarchy and Fordist corporatism.[57] The *gift of* [wh]at politics bestows on technique in the form of unflinching [techn]ology has a return on its investment: the perfection and [exten]sion of modes of control.

[W]hereas it may take months of ceremonies, mutilations, rites [and sh]ared existence to produce the inscription of sexual politics [in P]apua New Guinea, or the perpetual repetition of prayers, [pen]itent confessions in the great universalist religions, even the [lo]ng gradual inculcation of modes of thinking and doing in [lab]or apprenticeship – a few hours of daily exposure to self-[produc]ed pornography, sites of auto-surveillance and the flood

APOLITICS AND POLITICS

hegemonic effort is extended over everything, which intensifies domination above and beyond the ancestral walls of the City. This makes refusal all the more urgent, which can in turn bring about an unprecedented display of destruction, indoctrination and surveillance.

In the most 'advanced' countries today, the concentrated failure of colonialism, fascism, Nazism, Leninism and Stalinism has paved the way for the establishment of techno-democratic totalitarianism. This mode of domination, which cannot speak its name, only imperfectly broke with the distinctive features of absolutist regimes of oppression. Instead, it was proclaimed that we were in the moment 'after', effectively breaking numerous laws and customs, keeping valid what was necessary, but supposedly obsolete, now transformed into 'exceptions'. (This singular disposition pushed Agamben to declare, rather schematically, the universal state of exception.[53]) Local variations on techno-democratic totalitarianism abound and allow people of different nationalities to *personalise* their dictatorships. Fewer technocrats here, fewer neighbourhood watch communities there; more of the spectacular over here, more procedure over there. In addition, under the imperative of modernisation, the old system of free zones of society has been dismantled, and the instituted communities are becoming more and more suspect. They have to be replaced by panoptic associations. Common groupings found themselves on the outskirts of concentrated power, and their relative autonomy depended on adopting from within traditional obedience, tangential to constitutional regimes. The new 'social networks' no longer need to impose tradition as a coercive norm on their members, who can, one by one, establish themselves as petty tyrants with no other goal than propagating politics as a necessity, whatever becomes of it thereafter. Even though traditional communities by no means gravitated *towards* apolitics in their functioning, and although they constantly served to tame dissidents, their mere existence nonetheless signalled the limitations of politics. Their erosion, while diminishing some effects of old conformism, also had the consequence of discrediting the hypothesis of an outside.

Gracchus Babeuf, the ardent defender of 'liberty of the press' in the eighteenth century, helped to establish a discourse justifying the media that to this day continues to bolster all positions of its kind, even concerning the internet. However, beside the grandiose and real description of the benefits of publicised exchange, the future *Tribun du peuple*[54] had no qualms in recommending a grand system of informing, inspired by the ancient *bocca della verità*. His 'newspaper' was to be the 'letter box for all those charged with the surveillance of the homeland', and invited its readers to share in the best of its revelations.[55] Some time later, while in the US, Tocqueville noted how easy it is to block this media-covered apocalypse of truth ('*the only way to neutralise* the effect of the public *journals* is to multiply them indefinitely').[56] We still face similar difficulties, regardless of the different forms they take (written word, audiovisual, electronic and so on). Whereas the potential political truth content of journalism is getting harder and harder to recognise in the organised proliferation of brouhaha, community or horizontal policing, in contrast, so concomitant with the *phrase* of vigilant communication, intensifies a totalitarian and transparent politicisation in which anyone can shift from victim to executioner.

[14]

Techno-democratism appears as the final phase in s cidental progress, and it is a permanent catastrophe is not problematic in essence; its effects are what v It is not technology that truly rules – it is used as a point of being identified with the regime of the g speaking about a multiform *tekhnē* operating o governance to computer *operating* systems, from to the stuff of self-help, and that is put in place b of powers.

There are several stages. We must first circu trated government in its technical pomp (jur property codes, votes, administration and so o call *formal democracy* is here tantamount to a c regulated procedures that *become* democracy. detected in the United States but now tak goes hand in hand with a proliferation of lav expertise. The European Union, organised groups of uniformisation, is, in the capit lesque example of this transcendental bu standardisation – affecting production a tions in corporations, hospitals, schools as well as human gestures and the appe world (including the system of calibrati or the relation to thought in internet a the majority of experiences essential t cesses. Techniques of both governmer as *ends* – *indisputable* – in accordan ing that makes the limits of techni real. In a universe of finite possible of news produce you marvellously and, like never before, render you harmless. With the exception of techno-logy, getting one to conform [*l'acte de conformation*] depends on the quality of means used, its accomplishment remains rather aleatory, and its public is numerically quite small. In the *universal factory of the world*, what happens to us by way of mediatised technology is not only the massive expenditure of norms, the dissemination of parlance, it is also the rapid reprogramming of cognitive functions, the standard formatting of the brain. After having to connect and disconnect the cortex so many times, who doesn't feel dumber today than yesterday? In these different registers, the usual modes of capturing, studying, believing are always outdone: too slow, too rigorous, too contingent, indeed too superficial. Even the worst of television now seems like a gentle means that has survived despite everything: I am already nostalgic. I think we can bet on it: our future will continue to relegate the best the present has to offer to a number of moderately efficient methods. At the same time, every coercive system maintains at least a part of the preceding one and feeds off it in order to strengthen itself. We then have the great pleasure of fighting against more than one mode of programming.

Contemporary domestication is particularly relentless in creating subjects who are both *empty* and *occupied*. The rise of 'free' time in some societies must be understood in the context, which Marcuse understood, that saw a rise in control by way of consumption conjoined with greater surveillance by way of production, with a decrease in the number of hours spent at work.[58] Pascal saw the value of diversion [*divertissement*] via his metaphysical psychology.[59] In the techno*logical* era, everything indicates that diversion must make itself into entertainment or obedience to the *summons* of the contemporary (the demand to be of the times, to answer the phone, to *react* to the news, and to *follow* information ...). Organising distraction in this way is itself inscribed in the totalitarian politics of existence. Still, the cerebral *occupation* which results from it is only one side of a complex operation: it serves above all to make more acceptable a tendency towards mental *kenosis*, the self-emptying of the mind in order to better receive divine will. Today's globalised individuals owe it to themselves to lose all psychic reserve, namely the resistance of the manifested to its manifestation.[60] *I clear my head with a little physical exercise, flipping the channels, surfing the net. I keep my mind informed, I respond to the smallest change on my friends' internet accounts, sometimes I listen to music or watch a film, but nothing serious. To hell with critics, it's the little things in life that count.* Beside this circuitry of impulses and drives, today's *typical guy* amounts to very little, to these interjections of 'I mean', 'you know', 'like' that parse conversations and reflect the emergence, always kept at bay, of something other than emptiness.[61] For this new breed, *diversion is not necessary to forget death, it is necessary to forget life.* Such is the direction towards which the political prescription of the contemporary leads. Thus, in its technological part, the system of domination is not so much for the propaganda of this or that article of faith; it strives much more to justify its own omnipotence and its identification with the whole.[62]

[15]

The growing ascendancy of the techno-political is frightening; but it has not stamped out all other recourse. Politics follows from different forms of the political. A hoary if not forgotten modality will suddenly be called upon, even at risk of flagrant contradiction, if it carries an efficient solution and poses no threat to the institution. The analyses of power in the Marxist tradition have never admitted it, always surrendering to internal logic, to conceptual cohesion, and forewarning of the imminent collapse of capitalism as soon as the slightest contradiction arises. We saw it, yes, thank you. The political real is oriented by trends, it is neither limited nor defined by the coherency of its own system, which serves ultimately the order of the order, and, if necessary, logic be damned. Contemporary China can keep its bureaucratic structure, its old expansionist core with state-directed capitalism, as long as control is maintained (and, after some initial calibration, the internet will play the perfect auxiliary role).

The techno-political is largely supported by three previous modes of the political: the juridical, the theological and the military. The militaro-political, which promotes struggle against the enemy, was seen by Carl Schmitt as the oldest and the most determinant, to the point that he inscribed it into the very *Concept of the Political*.[63] This version sought to conceptualise Nazism at moments when interior and exterior enemies were designated; this would then be codified into a hysterical system of rules and mythologised as *Kampf*. Schmitt or no Schmitt, then, in renouncing the self-serving question of the original figure, we clearly see that the militaro-, the juridical- and the theologico-political keep good company with technological totalitarianism.

[16]

The military, the juridical, the theological, all of which express political ascendancy, are not synonyms for the army, law or religion – even less for war, justice or faith. In each of these three relatives, the sign is read as marking an alterity to politics – a mark increasingly indecipherable, and already ambiguous in other regions or times. Solitary or dyadic combatants, the great calls for retribution or punishment, mystical ecstasy, if not the fallacious ultra-world of living gods, all point to the possibility of a political insufficiency.[64] Armies, laws, cults and religions are the social institutions that complement, run alongside, at times affront or conceal the exercise of a collective reign. These institutions are political in that they legitimate the order *of* the order – and in that they seek to channel an instability that cannot be assimilated. Shamanism and forms of initiation have rules, protocols, a function in the group that authorises the violent projection into a magical space, the incursion into a mental vision (as in the 'Time of dreams' among Australian Aborigines), experiences that, in order not to be absurd or limitless, remain unsociable. The thirst for justice that no law, even divine, can satisfy was familiar to the Greeks – prior to deconstruction – in the figure of the female Erinyes, whose theological and normalising transformation into Eumenides (only after breathing new life into their fury on the stage of Athenian theatre) is told by Aeschylus. Thus, justice [*'la' justice*] does not consent to the excesses that provoke her, and regulates the pain of the wounded with the pain of the condemned. The wandering hero, the medieval knight on a quest, the samurai submit to divine commandments, an ethical code, a transcendence, *and* travel the world singularly constructing a *destiny* that in the end cannot be assimilated. Here and there, the non-political makes itself felt even under the pressure of its collective and nomothetic institutionalisation, which always runs the risk that it could very well reinforce the extension of powers that it elects, encourages and guarantees.

[17]

And so it also goes in relation to production, expenditure – and the economic. For me, the *type of economy* is only marginally affected by the modalities of the political, and vice versa. I mean that the militaro-political functions equally with a subsistence economy, mercantilism or neo-capitalism. Is it really the case that the theologico-political is encumbered by secularisation? It'll have to adapt, or manage to transfer the sacral, and so on. 'Capitalism' contributes to determining the forms of exploitation and liberation (by difference) through the dynamic process by which it organises work. It is hardly the case that 'ownership of the means of production' governs all oppression. Why would that be so? A passage from *The German Ideology* lays bare the idea that thousands of pages will readily pursue and that configures the essential of economism, well beyond Marx's inheritors. Human 'individuals', it states, 'begin to distinguish themselves from animals as soon as they begin to *produce* their means of subsistence'.[65] Consequently, what grants variety to their '*mode of life*' pertains to production. It doesn't go any further than that. In order to make the economy into a 'first cause', Marx and Engels need to find a human prerogative; to insist that production is limited to the activity of *homo faber*; to assume that nothing like organised sharing, tools or society exists among animals; and to brandish mysterious concepts (presumed materialist) such as 'productive forces' or 'life expression'. To be frank, I don't see in any of this anything that could hold up to theoretical examination, however cursory.

I do not deny the importance of the economy; I reject the determining relation postulated by Marxist and liberal analyses. The economy 'in general' is largely a political reality, even though behaviour, on the molecular level in particular, may adhere to its system — and despite the fact that it emerges through the perpetuation of the collective. When I speak of politics, I do not separate it once and for all from all public force, urbanism, the army and so on — neither do I subtract the economic component. We can easily characterise the 'democracy of capital' as an extension of control into the most remote recesses, then systematically re-write this text, replacing certain words with others; an exercise in style. That is precisely what I'm distancing myself from. The plasticity and relative liberty of wealth certainly allow for changes in social hierarchy, which traditional groups try to prevent (even if this well-known *mobility* never achieves the degree of the institutional *dream*). Empowerment appears as the consequence of virtual wealth; and everyone thus runs the risk of becoming an automaton of politics. In other words, the capitalist perspective *justifies* the political invasion and maintains it. The so-called totalitarian *regimes* are destructive variations that result from the political condensation of every instant and everyone, variations that push the movement right up to its mortal limit. Despite the rhetoric, their economic modes (corporations, collectivisation and so on) are tied no more than that to the absolute goals of government.

I said 'regimes'. They once took up the crux of the theoretical edifice inspired by Aristotle, and they form another way of transcribing politics [*ils sont une autre saisie des politiques*], giving a sort of precedence to the concentrated. A taxonomic inventiveness is advisable, which must take into account internal alignments, and we can speak of France, along with Mehdi Belhaj Kacem, as a *mediatised parliamentary democracy* [*démocratie médiatico-parlementaire*] (the prediction of its 'collapse' leaves me, however, undecided). This fragmentation of the analytical is the double consequence of the sophistication of contestatory discourses and the totalitarian expansion of politics: the more the latter controls space in its diverse regions, the greater the particularities created to demonstrate it. It becomes possible to interpret political life in a nation (or nations) as a bundled collection of distinct powers that intersect and converge.

[18]

The usual separations between public and private, collective and individual, dwelling and *polis* do not take into account the political effect that takes hold of the family, ordinary relations between people, or lifestyles. It is vain to believe that we have since lost these barriers and that contemporary discontent stems from the erasure of free subjectivity. The demand for *privacy* in general works as a political pulverisation at the level of affects – microfascism of repression, meek tolerance of the social-democrat and so on – and it goes admirably well with the techniques of control that were Victorian Puritanism or psychoanalysis.

Nonetheless, separating into categories like this does offer, by way of paradox, a possibility of relative autonomy vis-à-vis politics. Let us take Aristotle, who, while devoting himself to the totalisation of the *polis*, surreptitiously shunned the latter. The entire first part of *The Nicomachean Ethics* insists on the *architectonic* and *sovereign* place within knowledge of political science.[66] Ethics depends on politics. *Living together* (*suzēn, sumbioun*),[67] which characterises friends (or lovers, family) and presupposes a true shared existence, follows from an understanding of *living well* (*eu zēn*),[68] which Aristotle furthermore sets as the very goal of the *polis* both in the *Nicomachean Ethics* and in *Politics*. The purpose of Aristotelian ethics is well known: he is 'concerned most of all with *producing* citizens' of virtue oriented toward the *kalo-kagathon*, and the *good* of the City will transcend that of the individuals.[69] In the specific, culminating case of friendship the intention is equally clear. That is why the different sorts of *philiai* are compared to types of government, why friendship is indispensable in relations between citizens and so on.

And, suddenly, the movement takes a turn in another direction, revealing a different way of dividing ethics and the political. Whereas the science of government is by law superior to the study of morality, the knowledge of the latter establishes the content of the former. *Living well* allows *living together*, which in turn contributes to *living well* but is not entirely contained within it. In *Politics*, discussion of Plato's communism furnishes the occasion for Aristotle to affirm that an absolutely unified City would self-destruct.[70] Decidedly, living-with does not coincide with living-well. That *bios* and *zōē* take root in the City reveals the totalitarian ambition at work in politics. Ethical or daily life constitutively depends on the *polis*. Someone without a *polis*, an *apolis* human being, is an 'inferior' being.[71] The totality of life, from its nature to its content, from its form to its quality, is coextensive to the political thing. *And nonetheless*, the friendly or ethical excess comes to contradict the grandeur of its hold over life. I want to see here – both for and against Aristotle – the signs of a double language. The imperturbable philosopher is celebrating a *polis* governing all life and all of life. And in an unexpected move he sketches an outside, where life exceeds life; he also designates a structural resistance to the One of the *polis* – proof that in this traditional, theoretical edifice of politics an exit in the form of an escape hatch has been preserved.[72]

[14]

Techno-democratism appears as the final phase in splendid Occidental progress, and it is a permanent catastrophe. Technology is not problematic in essence; its effects are what we make of it. It is not technology that truly rules – it is used as a pretext to the point of being identified with the regime of the global City. I'm speaking about a multiform *tekhnē* operating on a range from governance to computer *operating* systems, from body-building to the stuff of self-help, and that is put in place by the ratification of powers.

There are several stages. We must first circumscribe concentrated government in its technical pomp (juridical guarantees, property codes, votes, administration and so on). What Marxists call *formal democracy* is here tantamount to a collectivity of auto-regulated procedures that *become* democracy. Juridicisation, first detected in the United States but now taking root elsewhere, goes hand in hand with a proliferation of law requiring technical expertise. The European Union, organised by commissions and groups of uniformisation, is, in the capitalist variant, the burlesque example of this transcendental bureaucracy. Generalised standardisation – affecting production and interpersonal relations in corporations, hospitals, schools, the street, on screen, as well as human gestures and the appearance of the objective world (including the system of calibrating fruits and vegetables) or the relation to thought in internet access – ends up codifying the majority of experiences essential to life into a series of processes. Techniques of both government and the self are imposed as *ends – indisputable* – in accordance with a circular reasoning that makes the limits of technique the boundaries of the real. In a universe of finite possible materials, every instrument, every standardisation, every computer function, every *enhancement* follows from human decisions that are both micro- and macro-political. Consequently, the computational hypothesis in cognitive sciences, which elucidates the neuronal by way of artificial intelligence, serves largely to present digitalisation as *natural* and *inexorable*, including any inconstructible portion. The equation of politics with technique does not however constitute a reduction of one to the other, as a reactionary interpretation might suppose (even if it would have the great merit of an all too rare denunciation). It is an opportunist strategy that attempts to give a specific form to totality under the guise of an indisputable universal. Techno-logy – it is indeed a question of a discursive act, or, more accurately, of a *phrase* – is a measure of the expansion of politics, spurred by the necessity of mastering revolutions and the growth of applied knowledge. Unionised, partisan or state bureaucracy, so maligned by Trotskyism and other movements, is a form of techno-political control. Burnham and Rizzi, if their writings do not live up to their first intuition, had the merit of recognising in the 1930s and 1940s the convergences of managing practices in Soviet-style planning, Nazi hierarchy and Fordist corporatism.[57] The *gift of self* that politics bestows on technique in the form of unflinching technology has a return on its investment: the perfection and expansion of modes of control.

Whereas it may take months of ceremonies, mutilations, rites and shared existence to produce the inscription of sexual politics as in Papua New Guinea, or the perpetual repetition of prayers, frequent confessions in the great universalist religions, even the slow and gradual inculcation of modes of thinking and doing in school or apprenticeship – a few hours of daily exposure to self-identified pornography, sites of auto-surveillance and the flood hegemonic effort is extended over everything, which intensifies domination above and beyond the ancestral walls of the City. This makes refusal all the more urgent, which can in turn bring about an unprecedented display of destruction, indoctrination and surveillance.

In the most 'advanced' countries today, the concentrated failure of colonialism, fascism, Nazism, Leninism and Stalinism has paved the way for the establishment of techno-democratic totalitarianism. This mode of domination, which cannot speak its name, only imperfectly broke with the distinctive features of absolutist regimes of oppression. Instead, it was proclaimed that we were in the moment 'after', effectively breaking numerous laws and customs, keeping valid what was necessary, but supposedly obsolete, now transformed into 'exceptions'. (This singular disposition pushed Agamben to declare, rather schematically, the universal state of exception.[53]) Local variations on techno-democratic totalitarianism abound and allow people of different nationalities to *personalise* their dictatorships. Fewer technocrats here, fewer neighbourhood watch communities there; more of the spectacular over here, more procedure over there. In addition, under the imperative of modernisation, the old system of free zones of society has been dismantled, and the instituted communities are becoming more and more suspect. They have to be replaced by panoptic associations. Common groupings found themselves on the outskirts of concentrated power, and their relative autonomy depended on adopting from within traditional obedience, tangential to constitutional regimes. The new 'social networks' no longer need to impose tradition as a coercive norm on their members, who can, one by one, establish themselves as petty tyrants with no other goal than propagating politics as a necessity, whatever becomes of it thereafter. Even though traditional communities by no means gravitated *towards* apolitics in their functioning, and although they constantly served to tame dissidents, their mere existence nonetheless signalled the limitations of politics. Their erosion, while diminishing some effects of old conformism, also had the consequence of discrediting the hypothesis of an outside.

Gracchus Babeuf, the ardent defender of 'liberty of the press' in the eighteenth century, helped to establish a discourse justifying the media that to this day continues to bolster all positions of its kind, even concerning the internet. However, beside the grandiose and real description of the benefits of publicised exchange, the future *Tribun du peuple*[54] had no qualms in recommending a grand system of informing, inspired by the ancient *bocca della verità*. His 'newspaper' was to be the 'letter box for all those charged with the surveillance of the homeland', and invited its readers to share in the best of its revelations.[55] Some time later, while in the US, Tocqueville noted how easy it is to block this media-covered apocalypse of truth ('*the only way to neutralise* the effect of the public *journals* is to multiply them indefinitely').[56] We still face similar difficulties, regardless of the different forms they take (written word, audiovisual, electronic and so on). Whereas the potential political truth content of journalism is getting harder and harder to recognise in the organised proliferation of brouhaha, community or horizontal policing, in contrast, so concomitant with the *phrase* of vigilant communication, intensifies a totalitarian and transparent politicisation in which anyone can shift from victim to executioner.

of news produce you marvellously and, like never before, render you harmless. With the exception of techno-logy, getting one to conform [*l'acte de conformation*] depends on the quality of means used, its accomplishment remains rather aleatory, and its public is numerically quite small. In the *universal factory of the world*, what happens to us by way of mediatised technology is not only the massive expenditure of norms, the dissemination of parlance, it is also the rapid reprogramming of cognitive functions, the standard formatting of the brain. After having to connect and disconnect the cortex so many times, who doesn't feel dumber today than yesterday? In these different registers, the usual modes of capturing, studying, believing are always outdone: too slow, too rigorous, too contingent, indeed too superficial. Even the worst of television now seems like a gentle means that has survived despite everything: I am already nostalgic. I think we can bet on it: our future will continue to relegate the best the present has to offer to a number of moderately efficient methods. At the same time, every coercive system maintains at least a part of the preceding one and feeds off it in order to strengthen itself. We then have the great pleasure of fighting against more than one mode of programming.

Contemporary domestication is particularly relentless in creating subjects who are both *empty* and *occupied*. The rise of 'free' time in some societies must be understood in the context, which Marcuse understood, that saw a rise in control by way of consumption conjoined with greater surveillance by way of production, with a decrease in the number of hours spent at work.[58] Pascal saw the value of diversion [*divertissement*] via his metaphysical psychology.[59] In the techno*logical* era, everything indicates that diversion must make itself into entertainment or obedience to the *summons* of the contemporary (the demand to be of the times, to answer the phone, to *react* to the news, and to *follow* information ...). Organising distraction in this way is itself inscribed in the totalitarian politics of existence. Still, the cerebral *occupation* which results from it is only one side of a complex operation: it serves above all to make more acceptable a tendency towards mental *kenosis*, the self-emptying of the mind in order to better receive divine will. Today's globalised individuals owe it to themselves to lose all psychic reserve, namely the resistance of the manifested to its manifestation.[60] *I clear my head with a little physical exercise, flipping the channels, surfing the net. I keep my mind informed, I respond to the smallest change on my friends' internet accounts, sometimes I listen to music or watch a film, but nothing serious. To hell with critics, it's the little things in life that count.* Beside this circuitry of impulses and drives, today's *typical guy* amounts to very little, to these interjections of 'I mean', 'you know', 'like' that parse conversations and reflect the emergence, always kept at bay, of something other than emptiness.[61] For this new breed, *diversion is not necessary to forget death, it is necessary to forget life*. Such is the direction towards which the political prescription of the contemporary leads. Thus, in its technological part, the system of domination is not so much for the propaganda of this or that article of faith; it strives much more to justify its own omnipotence and its identification with the whole.[62]

[15]

The growing ascendancy of the techno-political is frightening; but it has not stamped out all other recourse. Politics follows from different forms of the political. A hoary if not forgotten modality will suddenly be called upon, even at risk of flagrant contradiction, if it carries an efficient solution and poses no threat to the institution. The analyses of power in the Marxist tradition have never admitted it, always surrendering to internal logic, to conceptual cohesion, and forewarning of the imminent collapse of capitalism as soon as the slightest contradiction arises. We saw it, yes, thank you. The political real is oriented by trends, it is neither limited nor defined by the coherency of its own system, which serves ultimately the order of the order, and, if necessary, logic be damned. Contemporary China can keep its bureaucratic structure, its old expansionist core with state-directed capitalism, as long as control is maintained (and, after some initial calibration, the internet will play the perfect auxiliary role).

The techno-political is largely supported by three previous modes of the political: the juridical, the theological and the military. The militaro-political, which promotes struggle against the enemy, was seen by Carl Schmitt as the oldest and the most determinant, to the point that he inscribed it into the very *Concept of the Political*.[63] This version sought to conceptualise Nazism at moments when interior and exterior enemies were designated; this would then be codified into a hysterical system of rules and mythologised as *Kampf*. Schmitt or no Schmitt, then, in renouncing the self-serving question of the original figure, we clearly see that the militaro-, the juridical- and the theologico-political keep good company with technological totalitarianism.

[16]

The military, the juridical, the theological, all of which express political ascendancy, are not synonyms for the army, law or religion – even less for war, justice or faith. In each of these three relatives, the sign is read as marking an alterity to politics – a mark increasingly indecipherable, and already ambiguous in other regions or times. Solitary or dyadic combatants, the great calls for retribution or punishment, mystical ecstasy, if not the fallacious ultra-world of living gods, all point to the possibility of a political insufficiency.[64] Armies, laws, cults and religions are the social institutions that complement, run alongside, at times affront or conceal the exercise of a collective reign. These institutions are political in that they legitimate the order *of* the order – and in that they seek to channel an instability that cannot be assimilated. Shamanism and forms of initiation have rules, protocols, a function in the group that authorises the violent projection into a magical space, the incursion into a mental vision (as in the 'Time of dreams' among Australian Aborigines), experiences that, in order not to be absurd or limitless, remain unsociable. The thirst for justice that no law, even divine, can satisfy was familiar to the Greeks – prior to deconstruction – in the figure of the female Erinyes, whose theological and normalising transformation into Eumenides (only after breathing new life into their fury on the stage of Athenian theatre) is told by Aeschylus. Thus, justice [*'la' justice*] does not consent to the excesses that provoke her, and regulates the pain of the wounded with the pain of the condemned. The wandering hero, the medieval knight on a quest, the samurai submit to divine commandments, an ethical code, a transcendence, *and* travel the world singularly constructing a *destiny* that in the end cannot be assimilated. Here and there, the non-political makes itself felt even under the pressure of its collective and nomothetic institutionalisation, which always runs the risk that it could very well reinforce the extension of powers that it elects, encourages and guarantees.

[17]

And so it also goes in relation to production, expenditure – and the economic. For me, the *type of economy* is only marginally affected by the modalities of the political, and vice versa. I mean that the militaro-political functions equally with a subsistence economy, mercantilism or neo-capitalism. Is it really the case that the theologico-political is encumbered by secularisation? It'll have to adapt, or manage to transfer the sacral, and so on. 'Capitalism' contributes to determining the forms of exploitation and liberation (by difference) through the dynamic process by which it organises work. It is hardly the case that 'ownership of the means of production' governs all oppression. Why would that be so? A passage from *The German Ideology* lays bare the idea that thousands of pages will readily pursue and that configures the essential of economism, well beyond Marx's inheritors. Human 'individuals', it states, 'begin to distinguish themselves from animals as soon as they begin to *produce* their means of subsistence'.[65] Consequently, what grants variety to their '*mode of life*' pertains to production. It doesn't go any further than that. In order to make the economy into a 'first cause', Marx and Engels need to find a human prerogative; to insist that production is limited to the activity of *homo faber*; to assume that nothing like organised sharing, tools or society exists among animals; and to brandish mysterious concepts (presumed materialist) such as 'productive forces' or 'life expression'. To be frank, I don't see in any of this anything that could hold up to theoretical examination, however cursory.

I do not deny the importance of the economy; I reject the determining relation postulated by Marxist and liberal analyses. The economy 'in general' is largely a political reality, even though behaviour, on the molecular level in particular, may adhere to its system – and despite the fact that it emerges through the perpetuation of the collective. When I speak of politics, I do not separate it once and for all from all public force, urbanism, the army and so on – neither do I subtract the economic component. We can easily characterise the 'democracy of capital' as an extension of control into the most remote recesses, then systematically re-write this text, replacing certain words with others; an exercise in style. That is precisely what I'm distancing myself from. The plasticity and relative liberty of wealth certainly allow for changes in social hierarchy, which traditional groups try to prevent (even if this well-known *mobility* never achieves the degree of the institutional *dream*). Empowerment appears as the consequence of virtual wealth; and everyone thus runs the risk of becoming an automaton of politics. In other words, the capitalist perspective *justifies* the political invasion and maintains it. The so-called totalitarian *regimes* are destructive variations that result from the political condensation of every instant and everyone, variations that push the movement right up to its mortal limit. Despite the rhetoric, their economic modes (corporations, collectivisation and so on) are tied no more than that to the absolute goals of government.

I said 'regimes'. They once took up the crux of the theoretical edifice inspired by Aristotle, and they form another way of transcribing politics [*ils sont une autre saisie des politiques*], giving a sort of precedence to the concentrated. A taxonomic inventiveness is advisable, which must take into account internal alignments, and we can speak of France, along with Mehdi Belhaj Kacem, as a *mediatised parliamentary democracy* [*démocratie médiatico-parlementaire*] (the prediction of its 'collapse' leaves me, however, undecided). This fragmentation of the analytical is the double consequence of the sophistication of contestatory discourses and the totalitarian expansion of politics: the more the latter controls space in its diverse regions, the greater the particularities created to demonstrate it. It becomes possible to interpret political life in a nation (or nations) as a bundled collection of distinct powers that intersect and converge.

[18]

The usual separations between public and private, collective and individual, dwelling and *polis* do not take into account the political effect that takes hold of the family, ordinary relations between people, or lifestyles. It is vain to believe that we have since lost these barriers and that contemporary discontent stems from the erasure of free subjectivity. The demand for *privacy* in general works as a political pulverisation at the level of affects – microfascism of repression, meek tolerance of the social-democrat and so on – and it goes admirably well with the techniques of control that were Victorian Puritanism or psychoanalysis.

Nonetheless, separating into categories like this does offer, by way of paradox, a possibility of relative autonomy vis-à-vis politics. Let us take Aristotle, who, while devoting himself to the totalisation of the *polis*, surreptitiously shunned the latter. The entire first part of *The Nicomachean Ethics* insists on the *architectonic* and *sovereign* place within knowledge of political science.[66] Ethics depends on politics. *Living together* (*suzēn, sumbioun*),[67] which characterises friends (or lovers, family) and presupposes a true shared existence, follows from an understanding of *living well* (*eu zēn*),[68] which Aristotle furthermore sets as the very goal of the *polis* both in the *Nicomachean Ethics* and in *Politics*. The purpose of Aristotelian ethics is well known: he is 'concerned most of all with *producing* citizens' of virtue oriented toward the *kalo-kagathon*, and the *good* of the City will transcend that of the individuals.[69] In the specific, culminating case of friendship the intention is equally clear. That is why the different sorts of *philiai* are compared to types of government, why friendship is indispensable in relations between citizens and so on.

And, suddenly, the movement takes a turn in another direction, revealing a different way of dividing ethics and the political. Whereas the science of government is by law superior to the study of morality, the knowledge of the latter establishes the content of the former. *Living well* allows *living together*, which in turn contributes to *living well* but is not entirely contained within it. In *Politics*, discussion of Plato's communism furnishes the occasion for Aristotle to affirm that an absolutely unified City would self-destruct.[70] Decidedly, living-with does not coincide with living-well. That *bios* and *zōē* take root in the City reveals the totalitarian ambition at work in politics. Ethical or daily life constitutively depends on the *polis*. Someone without a *polis*, an *apolis* human being, is an 'inferior' being.[71] The totality of life, from its nature to its content, from its form to its quality, is coextensive to the political thing. *And nonetheless*, the friendly or ethical excess comes to contradict the grandeur of its hold over life. I want to see here – both for and against Aristotle – the signs of a double language. The imperturbable philosopher is celebrating a *polis* governing all life and all of life. And in an unexpected move he sketches an outside, where life exceeds life; he also designates a structural resistance to the One of the *polis* – proof that in this traditional, theoretical edifice of politics an exit in the form of an escape hatch has been preserved.[72]

That is what we have lost in the discourse of the majority that politicians today reflect and diffuse. When a point of distinction with ethics is hereafter observed, it is only a sub-case or a mere substitute. I wouldn't bet much on the eventual recovery of its autonomy once the dice have been thrown. Rather, I want to take up and increase these lines of fracture.

[19]

This apolitics would thus not be contemporary Italian philosophy's *'impolitico'*. I readily follow Massimo Cacciari when he stresses politics' inability to deliver what it promises,[73] but he stops short of the non-political, taking refuge in a 'radical critique of the political', in the 'work of deconstruction'[74] – refusing to accept the refusal. Cacciari's collective practice, two-time mayor of Venice, prompts us to think that he is reproducing in another way [*autrement*], by inverting values, an opposition between grand and small-scale politics, one becoming a partisan and sterile field, the other (at the municipal level) making itself into the governance of the plurality. The public office he exercised over the archipelago would still be the image of an involuted desire, turned towards the old figure of traditional, autonomous spaces. I equally appreciate that Roberto Esposito has relied just as heavily on the case of *'impolitico'*.[75] But I believe that he encloses the impolitical within the political once again, making the first the limit of the second.[76] The objective of non-reception may be summarised in these terms: 'the impolitical is not something other than the political, but only the political itself as seen from a point of view that "measures" it against something that it neither *is* nor can *ever be*: the political's impossibility. In this sense there is not really a duality, only difference.'[77]

No *refusal*, no *exterior*. Rather the demonstration of the logical and inherent flaw in politics to politicise (itself), all with an eye to a tacit double power in Cacciari or to a meditation on the powers of *life* or *a life* [la *ou* une *vie*] for Esposito, which therefore returns to politics. I am not differentiating myself just to isolate myself. I respect these *impolitical* attempts. I simply see them as continuing to refuse the postulation of an outside that could criticise the interior of the City. As if we mustn't go that far. Alberto Moreiras, one of the most astute readers of these theoretical propositions, calls for an 'infrapolitical practice', affecting the 'non-subject';[78] and he correctly sees the risk of a 'performative contradiction'[79] in any project promoting anti-politics. However, the consideration of an inferior space, which makes politics into the principal body of the text and of the infrapaginal political, cannot prove satisfactory. Here, too, we remain at the 'volume' full of the *polis*. Furthermore, the Heideggerian kernel that Moreiras maintains (the denunciation of a 'falsification of the world',[80] the belief in an *archi-Greek* conception of the City against the Roman *imperium*) is still up for much debate. And, in the end, apolitics is not limited to anti-politics.

As I revise this manuscript one last time, I am struck by the tacit agreement that my proposition may share with three other texts, all of quite different orientation, that I subsequently discovered; and, once again, I note a surreptitious political return or retraction. François Jullien, in his *Philosophie du vivre*, argues with an eye to something other than *life* [*la vie*], and his 'here and now'[81] seems close to the direction I want to take. Straight away he insists and repeats, 'to live is strategic' [*vivre est stratégique*], and I don't know quite what to make of this military commandment, of this 'political choice' that springs up.⁸² I would readily condemn along with Peter Sloterdijk (without however finding in it the same novelty of the times) the attempt at the modern eradication of 'what many had considered most valuable: the possible [*sic*] of distinguishing oneself radically from the world',⁸³ what is heralded as the 'politicisation'⁸⁴ of changing life. However, I am at a loss for words when confronted with his final description of the future ruled by 'universal co-operative asceticisms', peopled by 'workers on the consistently concrete and discrete project of a global immune design'.⁸⁵ In a few dense, elusive pages, Quentin Meillassoux in his turn announces: 'the end [*la fin*] of politics is the finality of politics, but the end of politics is not a politics [*une politique*]; life is not entirely within politics'.⁸⁶ I'd like to be able to endorse these lines. The invocation of 'life worth our humanity', the tedious equivalency between the 'unlivable' and the 'a-political', the generalising, conceptual tone however stop me in my tracks.

No doubt that since the refusal has to leave the laws of the City without going on forever without them, no evocation of apolitics will spread completely disengaged from it. This includes my essay, whose appeal, rhetoric, speech [*le parler*] are often *in conflict*, and thus possibly in full performative contradiction.⁸⁷ The difference, among those who want to think through the break with politics, arises from the moments of separation, from what is made of them, from what they are capable of opening up, and from the modes of their dissipation.

It is true that I am not far from contradiction. One could easily conclude that in saying that I am fighting for apolitics, I in fact betray this *refusal*, turning it into a militant activity. That in pointing to the outside of the total City, I am inferring a binary, one that can't escape the arena of organised combat. That in using these words to designate rapture erroneously reinforces the experience of being carried away. Emerging only in interruption, apolitics is neither permanent nor impermanence. It is possible that a call for refusal in the end only succeeds in reiterating the call; except that the utterance [*énoncé*] of the breach should be enough to stop it from closing up too quickly. Binarity is after all but one point of view, because I also refer to *non-politics*, *impolitics*, *anti-politics* and so on, as names that allow *a-politics* [l'a-politique] to take on meaning at the same time that they disrupt its *definition*, so necessary in a *dual*. With a work that speaks of the ineffable, the unnameable, it is not fully contained within its saying [*son dit*], which in turn affects its modes of investigation. If it is a question of politicising everything, it is not very difficult to subsume this text under unitary logic, to uncover an impossible failure – but what would we have really *proven* in all this, except the very hypothesis I want to break free of? If not, there still remains the question of contradictory thought, not insignificant or empty. Thinking's vulnerability to flaws, which also affects *indisciplined* branches of knowledge that work from positions of methodological lack and the limit points of knowledge, is already in play before this potential apolitics.[88] A restricted figure of rationality imposed itself in a certain line of thinking politics, just as in a certain politics of thought. It is up to us to beat it at its own game.[89]

[20]

More than during many eras, if such a thing may be said, it seems to me indispensable to rediscover the non-political expanse. Apolitics is a movement of critique, refusal, separation *and* proclamation where the actors, without losing sight of the fact that politics [*les politiques*] fights on their terrain, insist on the fundamental insufficiency of righting a wrong. It can be said that apolitics, seen in this way, is the luxury of sovereigns and the rich, for whom comfort is assured. One might ask: particularly in times of war or distress, don't other tasks come to the fore, pose greater urgency? But doesn't struggle that permits *fraternisation with the enemy* always go further and do more than the rejection of this or that war? The militaro-political serves the antiquated function of making soldiers walk straight, but it is not unstoppable at every step. – Some might still object that those who do politics are indifferent to all of this: 'you may leave, we're not going anywhere'. Despite the snide remarks, it is more or less certain that every one of my refusals reinforces the propensity of those around me to find the strength to say 'no'. Then, if I want to *change politics* [*changer de politique*], it is useless to believe in the virtues of passionate friendship or the possibilities of art. It is possible that politicians, the guarantors of order, even the most anonymous bystanders would not be disturbed by the appearance of an outside, but apolitics is not made *for the others* [*n'est pas faite* pour les autres]. Some might further ask: how then are we to believe in a conversion of the 'masses'? The auto-dissolution of politics via socialism, communism, classless society, oh, the project has passed. We are familiar with apolitics, we practise it, while at the same time we habitually say nothing about it, forget it.

'What you're talking about, then, is an aestheticism, an escapism?' No, if by that we mean to take our leave once and for all, or to cultivate the beautiful in one's tower, with no further concern for the outside than the occasional glimpse. Apolitics makes life more liveable. It does not guarantee subsistence, nor does it frame collective existence *tout court*, because it takes these concerns as its point of departure and then leaves them behind. *In principle*, life is not *liveable* for animals (which we are), it is simply *lived*. Politics, in its diverse meanings, holds to that, so that it might favour some or the greatest number of *lived* lives; disagreements then amount to oscillation, definition and technical qualifications (longevity) of who will live. Our contemporary *standards of living*, every *way of life*, the right to life or death, genetic modifications – none of that has to do with liveability. Today it is absurd to make a claim on politics that it cannot grant. At best, some civilisations might favour, more or less, but always indirectly, forms of exit from the political; rupture, separation have yet to be achieved, obstinately and singularly. At worst, 'the air-conditioned nightmare'[90] will recycle the air to breath, inciting us to keep the doors shut tight.

Notes

1 *Translator's note* (hereafter *TN*): Following what has become the norm, *la politique* is here translated as 'politics' and *le politique* as 'the political'. Note also that the original French chapter title, '*L'apolitique et la politique*', contains a homonym that cannot be rendered here in English.

2 Emmanuel Joseph Sieyès, *What is the Third Estate?* [*TN*: This is a paraphrase rather than a direct quotation. The text reads: '1. What is the Third Estate? *Everything*. 2. What has it been until now in the political order? *Nothing*.'], trans. M. Blondel (New York: Praeger, 1964 [1789]), p. 51.

3 The first description of apolitics that I published is in: 'L'apolitique de Maupassant', *Littérature*, 136, 2005, pp. 22–33.

4 Giorgio Agamben, *Homo Sacer: Sovereign Power and Bare Life*, trans. Daniel Heller-Roazen (Stanford: Stanford University Press, 1998). Robert Esposito, *Bíos: Biopolitics and Philosophy*, trans. Timothy Campbell (Minneapolis: University of Minnesota Press, 2008) and *Third Person: Politics of Life and Philosophy of the Impersonal*, trans. Zakiya Hanafi (Cambridge: Polity Press, 2012).

5 Jacques Rancière, *Disagreement: Politics and Philosophy*, trans. Julie Rose (Minneapolis: University of Minnesota Press, 1988) and *On the Shores of Politics*, trans. Liz Heron (London: Verso, 1995).

6 Michael Hardt and Antonio Negri, *Empire* (Cambridge, MA: Harvard University Press, 2000).

7 Jacques Derrida, *The Other Heading: Reflections on Today's Europe*, trans. Pascale-Anne Brault and Michael B. Naas (Bloomington: Indiana University Press, 1991); *Spectres of Marx: the State of Debt, the Work of Mourning, and the New International*, trans. Peggy Kamuf (New York: Routledge, 1994) and the collection: *La Démocratie à venir*, ed. Marie-Louise Mallet and Peggy Kamuf (Paris: Galilée, 2004). Chantal Mouffe, *The Return of the Political* (London: Verso, 1993).

8 Jean-Luc Nancy, *The Inoperative Community*, trans. Peter Connor, Lisa Garbus, Michael Holland and Simona Sawhney (Minneapolis: University of Minnesota Press, 1991).

9 Alberto Moreiras, *Línea de sombre: El no Sujeto de lo Político* (Santiago, Chile: Palinodia, 2006). Jean-Claude Milner, *Pour une politique des êtres parlants: Court traité politique 2* (Lagrasse: Verdier, 2011). A model for these *articulations* can be found in Nietzsche's *grand politics*.

10 On the contemporary path leading from anti-politics to *apoliticism*, see Laurent de Sutter, *De l'indifférence à la politique* (Paris: Presses Universitaires de France, 2008). For details on my critique of biopolitics, see 'De la vie dans la vie', *Labyrinthe*, 22, 2005, pp. 47–52 and, more fully developed, 'Leaving Politics: Bios, Zōē, Life', *diacritics*, 36:2, 2006, pp. 83–98.

11 Alain Badiou, *Metapolitics*, trans. Jason Barker (London: Verso, 2005), p. 116.

12 Alain Badiou, *Peut-on penser la politique?* (Paris: Seuil, 1985), p. 109.

13 Ibid., p. 93: 'l'interdit, à mon sens, [...] n'est pas une catégorie politique'. How convenient.

14 Ibid., p. 76.

15 Ibid., p. 76.

16 Ibid., p. 87.

17 For a more sustained and charitable presentation of this subject, see Bruno Bosteels, *Badiou and Politics* (Durham, NC: Duke University Press, 2011).

18 *TN*: By translating *parlure* by 'parlance', I am here following David Fieni's translation in Dubreuil, *Empire of Language: Toward a Critique of (Post)colonial Expression* (Ithaca, NY: Cornell University Press, 2012).

19 John Rawls, *Collected Papers* (Cambridge, MA: Harvard University Press, 2001), p. 482.

20 *For* the consensus, Jürgen Habermas, *The Theory of Communicative Action*,

trans. Thomas McCarthy (Boston: Beacon Press, 1987); *against* it, Rancière, *Disagreement*, and Gilles Châtelet, *Les Animaux malades du consensus* (Paris: Lignes, 2010).

21 [Confucius], *The Analects (Lun yü)*, trans. D. C. Lau (Harmondsworth: Penguin Books, 1979), II.3, p. 21. On the superiority of maintaining the social body over and above even the subsistence of the prince's subjects, see XII, p. 7.

22 On molecular and molar politics, see Gilles Deleuze and Félix Guattari, *A Thousand Plateaus: Capitalism and Schizophrenia*, trans. Brian Massumi (Minneapolis: University of Minnesota Press, 1987), especially ch. 9; and Guy de Maupassant, 'Philosophie-politique', *Gil Blas*, 7 April 1885 and 'Les Foules', *Le Gaulois*, 23 March 1882. I take the epithets of 'concentrated' and 'diffuse' from Guy Debord, *Society of the Spectacle*, trans. anonymous (Detroit: Black and Red, 1983), § 63ff (no page numbers); the 'spectacular' is for me but an extremely sly sub-case of an already sly politics.

23 On forms of resistance, see James C. Scott, *Domination and the Arts of Resistance: Hidden Transcripts* (New Haven: Yale University Press, 1990) and *The Art of Not Being Governed: An Anarchist History of Upland Southeast Asia* (New Haven: Yale University Press, 2009).

24 Frantz Fanon, *Black Skin, White Masks*, trans. Richard Philcox (New York: Grove Press, 2008 [1952]).

25 *TN*: Following David Fieni's translation of the author's *Empire of Language*, I translate directly the French *phrase* and *phraséologie* as 'phrase' and 'phraseology'. *Empire of Language* explains: phrase is 'a syntax of thought created *by* language, which concretised into *phraseology*' (7).

26 Carol Hanisch, 'The Personal is the Political' (1969) <http://www.carolhanisch.org/CHwritings/PIP.html> (last accessed 20 September 2015).

27 The current state of *indigenismo* has hardly changed from its elaboration fifty years ago: see Victor Gabriel Garces, *Indigenismo* (Quito: Editorial casa de la cultura ecuatoriana, 1957), p. 277ff.

28 Suzanne Césaire, 'Malaise d'une civilisation', *Tropiques*, 5, 1942.

29 Judith Butler, *Gender Trouble* (London: Routledge, 1990), p. 148ff.

30 Giovanni Gentile, *Ché Cosa è il fascismo*, I, 1, in *Opere complete* (Florence: La Lettere, 1990), vol. XLV, p. 36.

31 Ernst Jünger, 'Die totale Mobilmachung', *Krieg und Krieger* (Berlin: Junker und Dünnhaupt, 1930), pp. 9–30.

32 For the Frankfurt School, see, among others, Theodor Adorno and Max Horkheimer, *Dialectic of Enlightenment: Philosophical Fragments*, trans.

Edmund Jephcott (Stanford: Stanford University Press, 2002), p. 18: 'enlightenment is totalitarian'.
33 Simone Weil, *The Need for Roots: Prelude to a Declaration of Duties Toward Mankind*, trans. Arthur Wills (New York: Harper & Row, 1971), p. 120.
34 Against the use of totalitarianism, see Slavoj Žižek, *Did Somebody Say Totalitarianism?* (London: Verso, 2001).
35 Karl Popper, *The Open Society and its Enemies* (London: Routledge, 1945).
36 *TN*: Julien Coupat, founding member of *Tiqqun* and one of the so-called Tarnac Nine, was arrested by the French authorities in November 2008, accused of obstructing train tracks in what the French government labelled an act of 'terrorism'. In the controversy that followed, he remained in custody until May 2009 without formal charges being brought against him. In August 2015, Coupat was convicted of 'criminal conspiracy', the charge of terrorism having been for the time dropped.
37 Julien Coupat, 'La prolongation de ma détention est une petite vengeance', *Le Monde*, 25 May 2009.
38 Rancière, *Disagreement*, p. 139.
39 *TN*: On the night of 17 October 1961, French police in Paris massacred demonstrators protesting against the curfew targeting Algerians during the Algerian Revolution. It was not until 2012 that the French government, under François Hollande, recognised the 'bloody repression' of that night.
40 Jacques Rancière, *On the Shores of Politics*, p. 89.
41 Rancière, *Disagreement*, p. 137.
42 Rancière, *On the Shores*, p. 86.
43 Here I am drawing from my own 'Insurrection', *Labyrinthe*, 17, 2004, p. 25 and *À force d'amitié* (Paris: Hermann, 2009), V.8.
44 Ernesto Laclau, *New Reflections on the Revolution of our Time* (London: Verso, 1990), part I.
45 Jacques Derrida, *Politics of Friendship*, trans. George Collins (London: Verso, 2006), p. 236.
46 Chantal Mouffe, *The Return of the Political* (London: Verso, 1993), p. 3.
47 Slavoj Žižek, *The Ticklish Subject* (London: Verso, 1999), p. 191.
48 Jean-Luc Nancy, 'Finite and Infinite Democracy', in *Democracy in What State?*, trans. William McCuaig (New York: Columbia University Press, 2012), pp. 58–75 (p. 64 quoted here).
49 On what I call the 'inconstructible', see my 'Viral lexicon for future crises', *Qui parle: Critical Humanities and Social Sciences*, 20:1, 2011, pp. 169–78, and, more decisively, *The Intellectual Space: Thinking Beyond Cognition* (Minneapolis: University of Minnesota Press, 2015).

50 This paragraph is meant to supersede the formulation I first came to in the three-part 'trilogue' in 'L'interruption politique', *Labyrinthe*, 33, 2009, pp. 109–37.
51 Aristotle, *The Politics*, ed. Stephen Everson, trans. Jonathan Barnes (Cambridge: Cambridge University Press, 1988), I.2.1253a, pp. 13–14.
52 See Etienne Balibar's essay in *Marx et sa critique politique* (Paris: Maspero, 1979), p. 8. See also his essay: 'On the Aporias of Marxian Politics: From Civil War to Class Struggle', trans. Cory Browning, *diacritics*, 39:2, 2009, pp. 59–73. Gilles Dauvé's critique of politics is also relevant here.
53 Giorgio Agamben, *State of Exception*, trans. Kevin Attell (Chicago: University of Chicago Press, 2005).
54 *TN*: The name of Babeuf's newspaper after the Thermidorian reaction against the French Revolutionary Terror. Widely circulated, it ardently denounced the Thermidorians and later the Directory.
55 Gracchus Babeuf, *Journal de la liberté de la presse* (1794), repeated at the end of each edition (from 2 to 19).
56 Alexis de Tocqueville, *Democracy in America*, trans. Arthur Goldhammer (New York: Library of America Paperback Classics, 2004 [1835–40]), II.3, p. 205.
57 James Burnham, *The Managerial Revolution: What is Happening in the World* (New York: John Day Co., 1941). Bruno Rizzi, *The Bureaucratization of the World*, trans. Adam Westoby (London: Tavistock Publication, 1939).
58 Herbert Marcuse, *One Dimensional Man* (Boston: Beacon Press, 1964), p. 49, n. 38.
59 Blaise Pascal, *Pensées*, trans. Roger Ariew (Indianapolis: Hackett Publishing, 2005), L131, L139, L143, pp. 38–44.
60 'To live without a soul is the shortest and surest prescription for living long and in security in tyranny.' Vittorio Alfieri, *Of Tyranny*, trans. Beatrice Corrigan and Julius A. Molinari (Toronto: University of Toronto Press, 1961 [1787]), II.2, p. 83.
61 For a scathing 'reactionary interpretation', see Georges Bernanos, *La France contre les robots* (Rio de Janeiro: Editions France libre, 1946) or Michel Henry, *Barbarism*, trans. Scott Davidson (New York: Continuum, 2012 [1987]). See also Gilles Châtelet, *To Live and Think Like Pigs: The Incitement of Envy and Boredom in Market Democracies*, trans. Robin Mackay (London: Urbanomic, 2014 [1998]).
62 I develop some of this in 'Un sens de la réserve', *Labyrinthe*, 37:2, 2011, pp. 67–72, and 'Brève correspondance de l'écrevisse', *Pylône magazine*, 8, 2011, pp. 160–1, and in the second chapter of *Pures fictions* (Gallimard: Paris, 2013).

63 Carl Schmitt, *The Concept of the Political*, trans. George Schwab (Chicago: University of Chicago Press, 2008 [1932]).
64 On the militaro-political, see my 'Friends of War', *The Oxford Literary Review*, 31:2, 2009, pp. 175–87.
65 Karl Marx and Friedrich Engels, *The German Ideology* in *Collected Works* (New York: International Publishers, 1976), vol. 5, p. 31.
66 Aristotle, *Nicomachean Ethics*, ed. Roger Crisp, revised ed. (Cambridge: Cambridge University Press, 2014), I.2.1094a, pp. 3-4.
67 Ibid., IX.12, pp. 179–80.
68 Ibid., I.4.1095a, pp. 5–6 and I.8.1098b, p. 13.
69 Ibid., I.9.1099b, p. 15.
70 Aristotle, *The Politics*, II.3.1261a, p. 21 and 1263b, pp. 26–7.
71 Ibid., I.2.1252b, pp. 2–3.
72 Whatever one thinks of Leo Strauss, he is one of the rare commentators to identify what he calls 'a seeming self-contradiction of Aristotle's reading', one that extends to 'the trans-political, the supra-political [...] as the limit of the political'. *The City and Man* (Chicago: University of Chicago Press, 1964), p. 49.
73 Massimo Cacciari, *Della cosa ultima* (Milan: Adelphi, 1994), p. 299.
74 Massimo Cacciari, 'Nietzsche and the Unpolitical', in *The Unpolitical: On the Radical Critique of Political Reason* (New York: Fordham University Press, 2009), pp. 95–6.
75 Roberto Esposito, *Categories of the Impolitical*, trans. Connal Parsley (New York: Fordham University Press, 2015 [1999]).
76 Ibid., pp. xvi–xvii.
77 Ibid., p. xxi. For a genealogy of the impolitical, see his preface to the anthology, *Oltre la politica: Antologia del Pensiero 'Impolitico'* (Milan: B. Mondadori, 1996).
78 Moreiras, *Línea de sombra*, p. 237.
79 Ibid., p. 270.
80 Ibid., p. 237. Here Moreiras is referring specifically to Heidegger's *Parmenides*.
81 François Jullien, *Philosophie du vivre* (Paris: Gallimard, 2011), pp. 150ff.
82 Ibid., pp. 215, 219, 268.
83 Peter Sloterdijk, *You Must Change your Life: On Anthropotechnics*, trans. Wieland Hoban (Cambridge: Polity Press, 2013), p. 436.
84 Ibid., p. 369.
85 Ibid., pp. 451–2.
86 Quentin Meillassoux, 'L'Immanence d'outre-monde', *Ethica*, 16:2, 2009, pp. 67–70.

87 Ibid.: 'To think the non subject of the political is to be caught in a performative contradiction.'
88 On 'indiscipline', see my 'Défauts de savoir', *Labyrinthe*, 27:2, 2007, pp. 13–26 and *L'État critique de la littérature* (Paris: Hermann, 2009).
89 On the non-rational, see my *De l'Attrait à la possession: Maupassant, Artaud, Blanchot* (Paris: Hermann, 2003) and 'Des raisons de la littérature', *Labyrinthe*, 14, 2003, pp. 12–24, an article that may rely too much on philosophy.
90 Henry Miller, *The Air-Conditioned Nightmare* (New York: New Directions, 1945).

2

Liveable Interruption

[1]

The life that politics is concerned with follows the order: procreation, subsistence, direction. The sovereign still announces, 'I am master of myself as of the universe';[1] the contemporary individual learns to *manage* his or her existence and feelings. Salvation of life is but its prolongation in an ancestral biozoopolitics. But *each and every* life is mortal, outside of any and all politics. Whether it is *the patrimony, liberty – or death* – and even when *death lives* (¡*Viva la muerte!*), nothing political can alter mortality. When a body is kept breathing by the technico-medical machine, treatment only consists in postponing the announcement of an end. We may prolong existence because we're 'pro-life', give a social significance to a glorious or ignominious death, change the mode of accounting [*comptage*] by which the City counts lives (in demanding, for example, that from now on great apes, dolphins, parrots are *people*), include in human governance the preservation of the living (ecosystem, animal species, the planet); none of this changes, indeed nothing can change, the persistent political inability when faced with mortality. Solon observed that on this question no human is lucky. A banal remark, except that its author thereby relativised the scope of his constitution, which he nonetheless celebrated as necessary, a bulwark against the *destruction* of Athens by its own inhabitants.[2] Harmonious organisation assured that the *polis* would not perish by human hands; but this did not at all alter the luck of mortals.

[2]

In addition to the lived unfolding of existence, and faced with the mortality of us all, apolitics touches not on life [*la vie*] but on some life [*de la vie*] – that which is *liveable*.[3] Some life [*de la vie*]: life being there – and we could of course take up arms so that it may be delivered, guaranteed, nourished, all that the political organisation will allow – what makes of it some life I could live? [*qu'est-ce qui en fait de la vie la vie où je tienne*]? And not an *ordinary* life, and not only MY life? And then, in addition to being lived more or less well, what makes it liveable?[4] Since the lowest *level of life* can be liveable, and the highest standards of living might very well not be. It is in response to these questions that we may be able to frame apolitics in the largest way possible. Liveability would deteriorate if it were to become dogmatic; what concerns some life [*de la vie*] here may not concern some life [*de la vie*] there, whereas life [*la vie*] has indeed become a slogan, here, there and everywhere.

[3]

Politics does not have the force *to change life* [*changer la vie*];⁵ every promise of this type is the deadly motto of civic totality. On the other hand, *to change the living* [*changer le vivant*], vegetable and animal, is a long-standing practice, constitutive of human politics. Agriculture, from prehistoric times on, has produced genetically modified organisms: cows, wheat, horses, corn ... the list goes on. When it comes to prolonging or shortening individual life span, human order has demonstrated its competency, even though it remains limited by biological contingency and resistance. The *ways* to live or lifestyles are, for their part, forged by social forms, economic development and the regulation of force. If *to change life* implies a vast transformation of the fabric of life, which would get at the very heart of politics, that I'd like to see. *Change life*, proclaimed the propaganda of the French Socialist Party as early as 1977, and they were in no position to modify genomes. I find no irony in the dazzling existential transformation that, after 1981, a philo-communist then neo-capitalist then finally cleaned-up left managed to bring to a country that, obviously, had already arrived. I am less interested in *changing life*, here and now, through militant and government activity than in what that could possibly mean. In the collective, where each piece of the edifice is supposed to carry weight and occupy a certain place, this great change could only take place if it produced an elsewhere without any ties, and thus would not be of the City. Then, a party claiming to change life [la *vie*] would immediately declare that everything was continuing on the paths laid out yesterday, since life [la *vie*] in its performative definitions would be so greatly modified that some life [de *la vie*] would be denied in advance.

André Breton is surely the one to be credited with having brought the expression *to change life* into 'politics', an expression that had earlier appeared in *A Season in Hell*. In 1935, Breton had proclaimed, '"Transform the world", Marx said; "change life", Rimbaud said. These two watchwords are one for us.'[6] The formula in Rimbaud occurs in the pathetic and grotesque lament of a 'foolish virgin'[*vierge folle*], who, questioning her desire for an 'infernal bridegroom', begins to doubt: 'Does he have perhaps secrets *for changing life* [*changer la vie*]? No, he is only looking for them, I told myself.'[7] The internal dialogue, and the irony have the effect that this '*changing life*', put into italics by the poem, in the way of an incantation, a quote formed by these two words, appears as the distant announcement of a quest. In this search, Breton, like so many others, saw the 'alchemy of the verb'; I'm not so sure – that would mean we have to identify the infernal groom with the 'I' of the poem. In any case, this unaccomplished, imperfect mission for *changing life* transforms those who adhere to it, writes Rimbaud, into 'a serious danger for society', because they strive 'to escape from reality'.[8] Despite the links between antisocial escape and surrealist violence, the flat understanding of 'change life' and its designation as a rallying cry by Breton are tantamount to making Rimbaud toe the line, a pillaging of the apolitical resources offered up in his writing. As concerns life [la *vie*], everything leads us to think that the text of *A Season in Hell* challenges this overly general alteration in favour of a concrete poetics, one pervaded by *lives* and much more. A year before Breton, Simone Weil, at a time between renouncing Marxism and wandering towards sacrificial mysticism, took as her point of departure another line from Rimbaud, taken from the same text ('What a life! Real life is absent!'[9]). There she glimpsed that, in the 'so-called disinterested activities, [...]

in those moments of incomparable joy and fullness we know by flashes that true life is there at hand'.[10] She courageously announces, 'only fanatics are able to set no value on their own existence save to the extent that it serves a collective cause', and asserts a desire to go 'over the head of the social idol'.[11] The seeds were already sown however, because, running after 'the one' true life and announcing a return to the 'original pact between the mind and the universe',[12] Weil was already preparing her *regressio ad Deum*, by collapsing disgust at living and the 'obligation' for solidarity. At least in this other 'flash', alongside and at the same time as the Surrealists, at the height of the interwar period, a sudden desire for the apolitical arises, a desire that was not just renunciation.

[4]

Literature does not appear here by chance. Works of language are born in being ripped from silence, jargon, parlance, chatter, discursive regimes – and they respond endlessly to words that precede them, they depose the institution of phrases, and continue in a movement of hypercritique,[13] which does much more than simply oppose a thesis.[14] In that way, they participate in a form of refusal, an immense disagreement [*mésentente*] with the order of the order. Their self-affirmation (at worst, they exist, therefore, even under the extreme form of a nothingness of words) *can* be felt as an opening onto an outside. The fictitious real that literary texts provoke *can* then also redirect the virtue, necessity and intention of the order. The same goes for literature as for rebellions: in the act of separation, both are equally capable of reinvigorating the legitimacy of a political order as of proposing an exteriority to it. The work only takes on meaning through the experience of reading or writing, which can easily end up closing the apolitical potential – locking it up in civil interpretation, individual engagement, point-blank refusal or the end *tout court*, that instant where *we return to normal life*. Against reintegration, a desire to remain forever outside develops, a desire to climb to the heights of the 'ivory tower' that Sainte-Beuve named in reference to Vigny.[15] Vigny, to play on the words of a passage from his novel, *Stello*, could have preferred to put a 'hold'[*retenue*] on the flow of politics while simultaneously 'holding out' in deference to the Poet with a 'cranium of polished ivory'.[16] The structural independence of art articulated by Kant, and the autonomy of the ivoried (post)romantic creator are precautionary measures against the extension of the political domain made possible by the eighteenth-century revolutions. In an industrialised, 'democratic' and increasingly interconnected world, safeguarding marginal spaces at times seems tantamount to setting them aside in ever more radical ways.

And since it doesn't last, a discourse of complete politicisation of poetics arises in opposition, whose glorious century has just come to a close. Henri Meschonnic and Jacques Rancière, no doubt, strive to designate a supernumerary dimension to the four walls of the old *polis*, via the subject of rhythm and subjectivisation respectively. Both adhere, in passing, to the immense commentary of Victor Hugo and his 'Response to an act of accusation'. Both are constrained by their proper programmatic obsession to come back to customary frameworks. Meschonnic articulates the truth of an authentic 'politics' of the subject that, 'against the maintenance of order', in the end articulates no action other than itself (I'm not shocked, but is it really then a question of *politics*?).[17] Rancière, through the understandable desire not to limit himself to the 'politics of writers' where Sartre lingered, in the end comes to obliterate the said and the saying [*le dit et le dire*] of works, hanging on more and more to the 'institution' of literature (where, not surprisingly, one finds politics).[18] I find his historical montage of Belles-lettres prior to 1789 and the literature that follows no more convincing; furthermore, it has the irritating effect of placing, 'by principle', the entirety of texts coming out of Romanticism and the Revolution 'with' democracy. Rancière properly *inverts* a well-known position that was the outcome of the same poetic and political events – that is *l'art pour l'art*. Made into a 'doctrine', the proclamation of art for art's sake is eminently 'political', as Sartre had already established. However, it remains to be seen why these two conceptions (*l'art pour l'art*; democratic literature) coexist or why it is so easy to demonstrate both that the literary evades absolute political identification and that literature is always a political accomplishment.[19]

Confronted with this difficulty, Adorno proposed 'art's double character', distinguishing social-historical contingency from the negative, critical part that carries the work and is carried by it.[20] The breadth of these solutions is undeniable. In slightly altering [*détournant*] Nicole Loraux's reflections on Athenian tragedy, I would say that the literary act [*fait littéraire*], on condition that we don't define it *by* history, occupies a priori an anti-political place.[21] The place of literature *faces opposite* – literally *anti* – the City. This very particular place is assigned by the political body; its contours, its function vary according to different societies. To compare the regime of exception in Greek tragedy, although inscribed in the theologico-political of Dionysian rites, with the vast neutralisation of the literary in the globalised world, we can't help but note a growing tendency to marginalise the marginal – along with an empire of normalisation (which gives rise to the publishing market and theoretical arrangements, such as the conscious confusion of literature with storytelling). Literature is only tolerated from its position as anti-political space. It's a scandal when a writer rises up against the laws of the City. Or it's condemned to banality in advance, it is but literature.[22] Or, third option, it is driven to extinction, in the case where the exterior is not just minimised, but targeted for annihilation.

Anti-politics is a partial politicisation of the non-political. What is created in works – artistic or not – oscillates between these three instances. In the case of literature, some specific elements stand out (in particular the poetic as *response* to orders constructed via language), favouring the emergence of the apolitical. The apolitical can arise in addition to conceptual, historical, social, societal or discursive authority that the text may or may not amplify or validate; or alternatively it may come in the form of a description of the horrors of the City. The ambiguous *place* of the literary no doubt encourages us to probe for ways out; unless this place were granted precisely out of fear that the outside might prove too visible, too attractive (I have my suspicions). I would like to maintain that, in addition to its ambivalent inscription in and facing the City, literature also points to *potentialities* for apolitics, not systematically, not independently of what we make of them, nor for an eternal duration. Only sometimes, at certain moments, and by us.

[5]

Does what holds for literature extend to 'art'? Some configurations, some situations are shared; the gaps should relativise the general. It is accurate to stress how pale ordinary life is when juxtaposed to the raptures that a concerto may bring us to.[23] But other experiences, not originating from the arts, could be described in just the same manner – the highs in sports or gaming, orgasmic climax, the ecstasy of drugs. Thus, the absorption in a work of art is very much of *some lived life* [*de la vie*], not an absolutely distinct experience. We begin to speak *of art*, and we level the differences between the arts, between individual works. Nothing prevents us from thinking that the arts are born from a form of *crisis* (or from a crisis in the existing forms, which pushes us to create more). But does this tearing away amount to a *critique* every time, as Adorno claims? 'Through the new', neither 'critique' nor 'refusal' assert themselves every time.[24] In eliminating the heterogeneity of the arts and artworks, Adorno, against himself, ends in rationalising and mystifying. Art is summoned to *prove* the negative that should however keep this movement in check. From another, more empirical, point of view, does the breakaway critique, authorised by 'art', always appear the same or equal in all art forms, from music to architecture, the novel to sculpture? Finally, it doesn't follow from the diktats against 'industrial arts' that Adorno's piece of aesthetic theory couldn't, strangely, be equally applied, more or less well, to jazz, rock or comic books.

The arts, not all identically, not all the time, not under all their expressions, not automatically any more than other experiences are favourable to an exit from the *polis*. Sometimes they lead almost immediately back to a space of political tension where the savagery of the exterior is tempered, converted into figurative form, associated or denied. The architecture that materially erects the walls of the City is emblematic. Vauban built the fortifications for the power of absolute monarchy.

Le Corbusier attempted to collectively renew the monastery or public projects. Mies van der Rohe opened private sector work onto the spectacle of public life through the height of transparent towers and ensured that the one didn't communicate with the other. Michelangelo transformed stone steps into the flow of lava with the cascading staircase that finds itself winding up to the entrance to the Laurentian Library reading room. James Turrell made use of a crater formed by a meteorite in the desert of Arizona to create rooms of light. Thoreau put together the simplest of cabins on the shores of Walden Pond. Whereas these undertakings, which require mobilising human force and industry towards their goals, have an obvious and very common link with politics, their 'secondary' relation is without parallel: tangible adhesion (Vauban), revolutionary and utopian ambition (Le Corbusier), performative and perhaps distanced commentary (Van der Rohe), affirmation of an elsewhere within marginality (Thoreau), a hermetic non-place (Turrell), a *grandiose hic* (Michelangelo). Quite often, regretfully, ordinary architecture has nothing of the *secondary*. It is the product of official terms and conditions, without thought, at times with cut corners and a 'signature'. Along with this architectural example, we can think of a hundred others; a discourse on the inevitable and necessary apolitics of art would be like a pious vow, or, hollowed out, better yet a theoretical façade plastered onto the real.

[6]

The arts are not the privileged depositories of chaos. Naturally, there is order in art. The idea of creative spontaneous action that spanned the previous century could not entirely eliminate syntax, relations between notes and colours, anticipation of what follows (logic be damned). The idea according to which the rules of art *would correspond* to political norms is far too imprecise. No *happening* has set us free. Quite the opposite, the confusion between art and regulation (be it cognitive or social) is schematic and suicidal. Racine's alexandrine is more than two groups of six syllables, a Brandenburg concerto is more than the calculated stacking up of accords and counterpoints. The form is real, but the lightning effect of the work tends to obscure it, sometimes through overexposure of its own ordinariness. (This is not unique to art, the same could be said of other modes of thought.)

The momentary cancellation of the rules imposed by their application *could* serve as an *exemplum* of an exit from the *polis*. Marcuse proposed something similar when, in putting art on the side of a 'totally unpolitical medium' whose 'content becomes *meta*political', he affirmed paradoxical affinity with 'the revolution'. Because in both cases, he affirms, we seek to '"chang[e] the world"' through 'liberation.'[25] I am tempted by his hypothesis of a 'Great Refusal'[26] expressed through art. However, it seems that revolutions strive above all else to liberate the world and for the long term, whereas artistic experience liberates us from the world in an instant.

[7]

'Dadaism and surrealism made the mistake of associating liberation of lived poetry and the revolution of daily life.'[27] 'After all, it was modern poetry that, for the last hundred years, had led us there. We were a handful who thought it necessary to carry out its program in reality, and certainly to do nothing else.'[28] 'The surrealists, some of them at least, understood that the only worthy way to overcome art was through life.'[29] 'The role of the Situationist as professional amateur and anti-specialist remains a specialisation up until the moment of economic and mental abundance when everyone becomes an "artist", in the sense that artists have yet to attain: the construction of their own life.'[30] 'SI [Situationist International] had from the outset been a project much vaster and deeper than a simply political revolutionary movement.'[31] 'What was expressed in May 1968 with the lucidity of an abrupt and brutal revelation is nothing other than the refusal of the afterlife in the name of life.'[32]

Voiced between 1960 and 2008, these reflections on a past, present and future practice point to the scale of the Situationists' ambition and misunderstanding. The supersession [*dépassement*] of politics would also be the 'supersession [*dépassement*] of art',[33] by a perspective 'perforce avant-garde',[34] following Dada and surrealism. A quadraphonic changing of life: in poetry; in social struggle; in an active critique rooted in 'overturning' [*renversement*], 'deturning' [*détournement*] and 'insurrectionary style';[35] and, finally, in everyday life. In many ways, the Situationists scratched the surface of the notion of apolitics via a militancy that, in a few rare instances, took aim at the 'suppression of politics'[36] via revolution. Despite some declarations to the contrary, Situationists did not change the facts of politics, nor the fact that politics must *reign*. The violent denunciation of the spectacle still makes sacrifices in the name of plenitude and totality, through an inability to capture the outside of the *polis*; it leaves in place the frame of the frame. The watchword of overcoming art, which keeps the organisation intact, serves as an excuse first and foremost to collapse lived totality onto the order of struggles. Thus, in the 1960s, the *Internationale Situationniste* 'strives to illuminate and *coordinate* the gestures of refusal and the signs of creativity',[37] or promises '*unified* critical theory'.[38] The failure of the political overflowing of politics would lead, for both Guy Debord and Raoul Vaneigem, to a revalorisation of art understood as *life* [*la vie*]. Individual life for the former, who, attacking the latter in 1972, said, 'a book's beauty can be judged only by that of its author's life',[39] and apparently believed that his time on earth deserved more than one 'panegyric'.[40] And as for Vaneigem, he opted for the life of energetic and spontaneous vitalism, and at the time was naively fascinated by 'woman and child'.[41] Very strange. It would probably be best to leave these shores behind us.

Can we emancipate ourselves from political emancipation, as the calls for 'overcoming' seem to indicate? That remains to be seen, but we'll first have to make a detour by way of lived liberties.

[8]

Living from birth within a collectivity that I didn't elect and that breathes life even into this me that is not I, this I that is not me, I've come to find in such an arrangement the ultimate guarantee of a sustainable plurality. Coercion runs throughout politics, it sews together the very threads of social fabric. It is as indispensable as it is unbearable, and the fact that it is necessary if one is to accomplish 'the noblest ideals' makes it odious in direct proportion. The *libido dominandi* is largely the consequence of an exercise in possibilities: place creates desire. An a-centric organisation, a tangible, concrete rhizome without hierarchy makes up the great fantasies of praxis. Such fantasies originate in the extrapolation that comes from the desire to restrict and coalesce powers before arriving at a vision of the human world completely without ties. The social arrangement is falling into ruin, and it follows conclusively that domination ceases when politics stops – indeed that this interruption is precarious but it exists.

Liberation is in this sense 'produced' both through organisation, a compensation acquired at a steep price (this is the give and take described by classical political philosophy), and through resistance to the powers of organisation (according to the figure privileged by a revolutionary or 'radical' posture). Humans are not 'born' free. At best, a 'free space' is reserved for them, which is not the same thing. The logical and chronological primacy of power passes for the expression of a pessimism of action. That is debatable, because to posit an alleged liberty at the start, we'd have to consider that it has been lost, corrupted, distorted at every show of force [*coup de force*], and admit a destructive functioning within the very structure of society. But the fact that liberation is a product of the ordering of order does not mean that it only takes shape there. In order to make ourselves heard, we, the black slaves supposedly mute, have to struggle against the system of rules, and a great distance separates subjugation from the construction of a subject.

The primacy of domination does not make it *more* political than liberation. It is expected that domination be contested: 'one doesn't rule over stones'. Or, in other words, 'power' and 'coercion' are named from a place of implementation and presuppose bodies that serve both as obstacles and as targets. The gesture of extricating oneself from constraint can afford the chance to apprehend a place other than this place [*un autre lieu que ce lieu*], and in this way would be *more* apolitical.

The moment of liberation creates a snag, breaking a few strings that currently keep us tied up in this government, this oppression. Political liberation is not fundamentally distinct from liberation from politics. Both cases pose the question of rupture and the possibility of an event, with the closely related prospect of being brought back within the fold (treason, legalisation, (re-)memorialisation), which would require starting over if we are looking to validate the gesture of deliverance or to enlarge the space. (The famous social-benefit-seized-in-grand-struggle, that Trotskyists see everywhere, is simply the repercussion of liberation, the result of the moment when we reached an understanding to *stop* the process of emancipation.) But a *political* refusal targets specific public behaviour, it bans de facto any assent to an exterior. Like domination, it speaks *in the name of others*. In many situations, pronouncing a certain 'we' is an act of bravery that either brings to the fore or displaces this or that ignored category, held in contempt by the organisation of the *polis*: the people, slaves, blacks, women, homosexuals, Jews, Arabs, proletariats, the undocumented, the young, the homeless, animals and so on. This 'we' is to be filled up, occupied by those who were not the 'first signatories', and each new start accomplishes an interruption in the previous condemnation or censorship, one that may go beyond just assigning identities. I don't deny the glory, courage or beauty. Nonetheless, this unconditional can be strictly framed. The oppressive realism of taking up action is perceptible, and leads to questions such as 'can a white man speak about a subaltern black woman?'[42] The question is inept to the degree that it obstinately ignores the volatility of a critical and emancipatory 'we', and from the start mistakenly takes it for an antiquarian system of classification based on bodily traits. At the same time, it *carries* [*porte*] – going beyond the polemic will of those who give it voice. If I take up the phrase 'we, the people', identifying myself with it, I thereby recognise that someone has spoken in my name and rightly so. If I begin with 'we, the young', I name in advance others whom I will never know.

In apolitics, I do not target 'the-others' [*les-autres*], nor do I make claims in 'the name of the anonymous'. I can try to exit the enclosure of the *polis* 'for others' than myself, in the sense that what I do inspires or ignites. But what of 'the' others? We also exist outside of politics by the strength of our affect, but it is indeed 'us' rather than 'we, lovers'. I write for those who read me, not just anyone, nor could it be otherwise, those who become me only by not being so, who turn as much as possible towards this improbable 'we' without qualities. A liberation from politics would not at all free us from the 'hell' that would be 'others' [*les autres*]; momentarily, it suspends the external instance of their nomination, it forgets to call roll or to make the call [*faire l'appel*]. Thus, yet another thing it shares with the experience of works of art.

[9]

Domination only holds if I bear and support it, as in: inverting perspective, revenge and especially the wretched oppressing the more wretched – my illiterate grandmother, orphaned and ridiculed, would brandish a cudgel to make the dog obey. We should expect to find the powers traversing and maintaining the organisation of society in all of its actors. Globalising technological capitalism has the strength a priori of not leaving any position outside its coercive reach. If a rich, influential white man is supposed to benefit from a larger 'playing field' than a minor worker in the Third World, uprooted from his rural environment and transposed to a sordid factory, then the conventional vulgarity that the majority of the powerful demonstrate in the production of their desires indicates in fact just how subjugated they really are. Domination passes by way of humans who receive and emit it; it has multiple relays such as its institutions, establishments and outposts. In contrast, liberation, although similarly accomplished and transmitted in the concentrated or the diffuse, cannot take objective form without losing its intensity or taking on some qualifier. Every 'liberty' is as much a rallying cry as it is the amplification of a resistance. The programme for liberation is not about to let itself be cut short. The total reduction of our lives to these battles, is that what you want? One can, following Blanqui, chant 'No gods, no masters'; and, in the same gesture, it would simply be a matter of throwing oneself into the articulation of a 'purely military ... program' demanding 'organization' on every page, with different ranks, compulsory operations, separated disciplines and idiotic oaths ('I swear to fight to the death for the Republic, to obey the bosses' commands, and not to stray from the flag even for a single moment').[43] Well, that's that. For all his faults, Max Stirner still saw clearly, two decades before Blanqui, that 'political liberty means that *the polis*, the State, is free [...] It does not mean *my* liberty, but the liberty of a power that rules and subjugates me.'[44] Anarchists, *encore un effort!* given that the critique led Stirner to equate 'my power' and 'me';[45] we still need to rid ourselves of such emancipation. I'd like another, greater liberation [*une libération de plus*].

[10]

Nothing is apolitical but experience. Apolitics is neither guaranteed nor durable. How peculiar are those humans who, despite being informed of the three little tours of duty they have to complete, rush to repeal the evanescent. Politics functions by *flashes*. But, just like a drug, coming down is not always pleasant. We need to cultivate a form of inebriation that we can return to again and again without languishing away in lethargy and stupor. (Marxists despise drugs since they impede 'consciousness raising'. These Marxists are all too serious. True, the obsession of addicts who give themselves over to automatism and the search for the next fix is admittedly far from an ideal. As it stands, the desperate junkie goes a long way in offering up a mirror image, only slightly exaggerated, of the American hooked on supermarkets – voracious, elated, empty. Nonetheless, it can happen that, out of disdain for mundane matters, one becomes a vein to stick or a lung to fill – and that in this alcoholic drunkenness, this collapsing of the senses, we experience another world.)

Strictly speaking, apolitics designates a specific experience giving access to the non-political, an experience that affirms both refusal and designation. *No object, no person, no event, no discourse, no work of art is apolitical through and through.* Neither is the *same* thing (thought, emotion, injection, construction, colour) apolitical for all and forever. I have the impression that more and greater things are at stake in this rush than the duration of instituted dreariness. I do not want then to set myself the task of counting spheres, isolating one from another: thought, art, science, religion and who knows what else. Politics does all it can to rule over everything or almost, whereas almost everything could at times cede.

[11]

The rise of a radial refusal, radiating out from a common dissatisfaction – without a programme, without a party – does not leave the equilibrium of powers untouched. If it is true that apolitics, in setting up organisational goals, loses some of its vibrancy and gains an adventitious efficiency, its simple diction already lends itself to limiting the scope of such a hold. The amused indignation, scandal and rage that the refusal of politics provokes are remarkable. It is enough to talk about it here and there and the tone starts to rise, I've grown used to it. Insults are thrown, mockery is heaped on – 'you must be quite happy to have found society, then, no? But, in any case, it couldn't work. What are you still going on about? No, no, no.' The reaction is such that even if the hypothesis of apolitics were proven null and void, I would still want to push it forward, if nothing else just to see what happens. I continue to hold that this rejection of the rejection speaks the unspeakable, a prohibition more than a verdict on coherency and exactitude. That censorship crops up, even among the fierce proponents of liberty, points to the intensity of the recruitment process that from this point on we are assigning ourselves.

For me, I who refuse and declare, 'here is something else', every discussion, every lampooning provides a chance to create the space of an interruption, and, by way of that, encourage new secessions. Live, better [*Vivre, mieux*]. Indeed, go after this myriad of flashes, dazzling enough for the power holders, of which we are also a part. I am unflagging and, at times, annoying. Why this, why that? Some opt for a negative heroism, their gestures held up for others to contemplate, not to be reproduced but extended, prolonged. Volume II: to write and be written [*à écrire*].

Notes

1 Pierre Corneille, *Cinna*, in *Six Plays by Corneille and Racine*, trans. Paul Landis (New York: The Modern Library, 1959), p. 120. *TN*: translation modified. The original reads: 'Je suis maître de moi comme de l'univers.'
2 Solon, *Poetarum Elegiacorum Testimonia et Fragmenta*, trans. B. Gentili and C. Prato (Leipzig: Teubner, 1988), vol. I, fr. 3, pp. 102–5, fr. 9, p. 14.
3 *TN*: The distinction between *la vie* and *de la vie* is here, following the author's suggestion, rendered as 'life' and 'some life' respectively.
4 See my *À force d'amitié* (Paris: Hermann, 2009), which throughout develops a way to make one's life liveable.
5 *TN*: This is a reference to the Rimbaud poem quoted below – 'to change life' and 'changing life' are here used interchangeably and both refer to Rimbaud's *'changer la vie'*.
6 André Breton, 'Speech to the Congress of Writers', in *Manifestoes of Surrealism*, trans. Richard Seaver and Helen R. Lane (Ann Arbor: University of Michigan Press, 1969), p. 241.
7 Arthur Rimbaud, *A Season in Hell*, *'Delirium, I. The Foolish Virgin'*, in *Complete Works, Selected Letters*, trans. Wallace Fowlie (Chicago: University of Chicago Press, 1966), pp. 186–93 (p. 189 quoted here).
8 Ibid.
9 Ibid., p. 187.
10 Simone Weil, *Oppression and Liberty*, trans. Arthur Wills and John Petrie (London: Routledge, 2006 [1958]), p. 104.
11 Ibid., p. 124.
12 Ibid.
13 For more on hypercritique, see my *L'État critique de la littérature* (Paris: Hermann, 2009), III.
14 Theodor Adorno: 'Art is the social antithesis of society.' *Aesthetic Theory*, trans. Robert Hullot-Kentor (Minneapolis: University of Minnesota Press, 1997), p. 8.
15 Sainte-Beuve, 'À M. Villemain', in *Pensées d'août: Poésies* (Paris: Renduel, 1837).
16 Alfred de Vigny, *Stello: A Session with Doctor Noir*, trans. Irving Massey (Montreal: McGill University Press, 1963 [1832]), ch. XIX, p. 66.
17 Henri Meschonnic, *Hugo, la poésie contre le maintien de l'ordre* (Paris: Maisonneuve & Larose, 2002).
18 Jacques Rancière, *The Politics of Literature*, trans. Julie Rose (Cambridge: Polity Press, 2011), p. 3. See also his *Mute Speech*, trans. James Swenson (New York: Columbia University Press, 2011).

19 For further refutation of Rancière, see my 'What is Literature's Now?', *New Literary History*, 38:1, 2007, pp. 43–70.
20 Adorno, *Aesthetic Theory*, pp. 5–6.
21 Nicole Loraux, *La Voix endeuillée: Essai sur la Tragédie Grecque* (Paris: Gallimard, 1999), ch. 3.
22 *TN*: The latter half of this sentence plays on Verlaine's poem 'Art poétique', whose last line reads, 'Et tout le reste est littéraire.'
23 Adorno, *Aesthetic Theory*, p. 16.
24 Ibid., p. 22.
25 Herbert Marcuse, *Counterrevolution and Revolt* (Boston: Beacon Press, 1972), III.5, p. 104.
26 Herbert Marcuse, *One-Dimensional Man* (Boston: Beacon Press, 1964), pp. 63ff, 70, 255. See also Maurice Blanchot, 'Refusal', in *Friendship*, trans. Elizabeth Rottenberg (Stanford: Stanford University Press, 1997 [1958]).
27 Raoul Vaneigem, 'Terrorisme ou révolution', in *Pour la révolution*, ed. Ernest Coeurderoy (Paris: Champ Libre, 1972), p. 19.
28 Guy Debord, *Panegyric*, trans. James Brook (London: Verso, 2004), p. 22.
29 Raoul Vaneigem, *Traité de savoir-vivre à l'usage des jeunes générations* (Paris: Gallimard, 1967), I.XII.2.
30 Guy Debord, *Revue de l'*Internationale Situationniste (Paris: Fayard, 1997), 4 June 1960, p. 146.
31 Guy Debord, *The Real Split in the International: Theses on the Situationist International and Its Time, 1972*, trans. John McHale (London: Pluto Press, 2003), § 41, p. 58.
32 Raoul Vaneigem, *Entre le deuil du monde et la joie de vivre: Les Situationnistes et la Mutation des Comportements* (Paris: Gallimard, 2008), p. 16.
33 Debord, *Society of the Spectacle*, trans. anonymous (Detroit: Black and Red, 1983), § 191.
34 Ibid., § 190.
35 Ibid., § 206.
36 Debord, *Revue de l'*Internationale Situationniste, 2 Dec. 1958, p. 41.
37 Debord, *Revue de l'*Internationale Situationniste, 9 Aug. 1964, p. 388 (my emphasis).
38 Debord, *Society of the Spectacle*, § 211 (my emphasis).
39 Debord, *Real Split*, Annex 1, p. 95.
40 *TN*: Debord published *Panegyric I* in 1989 and *Panegyric II* in 1997.
41 Raoul Vaneigem, *Nous qui désirons sans fin* (Paris: Le Cherche Midi, 1996), p. 89. See also, *Entre le deuil du monde et la joie de vivre*, pp. 70–1.
42 See Gayatri Chakravorty Spivak, 'Can the Subaltern Speak?', in *Marxism*

and the Interpretation of Culture, ed. C. Nelson and L. Grossberg (Basingstoke: Macmillan, 1988), pp. 271–313.
43 Auguste Blanqui, *Instructions pour une prise d'armes* (Paris: Société encyclopédique française, 1973 [1866]).
44 Max Stirner, *The Ego and his Own: The Case of the Individual Against Authority*, trans. Steven T. Byington (London: Verso, 2014), pp. 127, 242.
45 Ibid., p. 242.

3

Forms of Experience

[1]

That politics seeks to capture the space of life suggests that apolitics has no place. Utopias are the places of no place. During the European Renaissance, part of the fragmentation of the collective that marked the Middles Ages disappeared in favour of concentric governance. This moment enabled the success of the word 'utopia', put forward by Thomas More. The place that doesn't exist at all, by the simple fact of its appellation, asserted itself as a point of reference in political thought. More did not invent the project of describing a different world, but the fate of his book propagated its malleable image, as well as the long shadow that went along with it. The *Utopia* event, which surpassed the treatise as such, is far from unitary, and I will only sketch out a few points: Utopia is not of this world; it represents a tearing away from contemporary politics, under the guise of its differences; it comes to fill in for a relative loss of marginal spaces; it thus takes a place left empty while also emptying out places; it represents the perfection of politics, which is no longer politics as usual; in this way, it is paradigmatic of all possible reform. These propositions could be set one against the other, or coordinated in a great sophism, a beautiful dialectic, or laid out as a tangled mess for those who dare enter. Utopia is as much the chance of an outside as its foreclosure. In its subsequent development, it has served more to extend boundaries and to launch again and again a plurality of politics, by inspiration or indifference. In announcing its inexistence ('u', the first letter of the word, transcribes the Greek '*ou*', a 'no'), utopia tacitly calls out for its actualisation, an undertaking that the Enlightenment would take on, in the same way that Ledoux built architectural ideals that would comprise the background of Italian paintings. Because utopia is *eutopia*: entering into competition with the *locus* of politics, it strives to be the exact expression of politics, or its slightly embellished reflection. On this point, the source of the refusal is dissolved in the exaltation of the best *polis*, and thus it no longer puts much into question. It builds off what Michel Foucault in a well-known conference termed 'heterotopias', both authorising a coherent 'no' *and* framing it within a description of the best *polis*.[1] In the aftermath of this surreptitious repoliticisation, the common slur of 'utopian' doesn't designate an exit, any exit. Rather it serves to disqualify either the evocation of the *polis* to come, which glistens in a distant future, or the effort to settle the terms here and now.

Utopian socialism neither holds itself to descriptions in books nor does it wait for the global metabole to introduce the new. It created Fourier's *phalanstères*, coffee shops, the '*commune*' amid arid lands, the countryside or within cities. 'Utopian' designates the chord struck between the project and the event of More's book. We'd be more accurately concerned with 'revolutionary heterotopias'. These places – where uses, customs and relations to molar and molecular levels reinvent themselves – *can* be favourable to apolitical experience, since they take as their point of departure the refusal of what exists, question practices and affirmatively break rank. But isn't it the case that they collapse under the weight of their institutionalisation? That they are erected and collapse, that is not the worst of catastrophes, the attempt maintains its value. However, we have to question the political *orientation* of these revolutionary heterotopias, which have tolerated colonialism (the Saint-Simonians were quick to settle Algeria) or have relied a little too much on 'the coming insurrection[*l'insurrection qui vient*]'.[2]

The eventual apolitical contribution is allotopic and atopic. The Greek '*heteros*' refers more to difference between two, the other of the same and of the other. 'Heterotopia' designates in fact this otherly world that inverts or modifies. '*Allos*' is other than this other, and if we had to situate the apolitical, it would be there.[3] It is possible that our conceptions of common space are so politically saturated that an outside must be understood as a place that is no place. The privative prefix alpha would not announce inexistence, rather it would indicate the negativity – *for* the *topos* of politics – of what is not contained in it. That is to say, the partial recovery of the propositions of a utopia, which, in its suggestive force and the ambiguity of its meaning, will repeat itself, designating by way of contradiction. The political *en*topia, claiming that all lies inside its domain, cannot tolerate the designation of an outside, this exit towards the other world where, alive, we would not remain.

[2]

Is Plato's *Republic* a utopia *avant la lettre*? I would say it is more than that, it is also that. Socrates insists that the City he describes to his interlocutors does not exist, that it is nowhere on earth. He does however locate it: it 'has its place in speeches'.[4] Thanks to this, other thoughts enter in surreptitiously as supplements – 'hard but in a way possible'.[5] The whole thing starts to totter when an amused Socrates comments, towards the end of the dialogue, that a 'sensible' person should not even try to get involved in politics. And even more tenuous, I would argue that we could translate it simply as every person 'endowed with a mind';[6] in short, one would have to be a chicken with its head cut off [*un oiseau sans tête*] to throw oneself into public life.

Plato's book contains the Utopia event in this delicate arrangement of heterogeneous postulates. A facetiously paranoid reading inspired by Leo Strauss might see a ruse against persecution ('ah, you know me, I don't get involved in politics') that is able to put forward a programme for governance that could not be heard in Athens.[7] Unless, that is, distaste for the victorious 'masses' doesn't put a stop to *speculative* practices on politics; a third possible interpretation would be that this way of theorising without relation to the real is a critique of the cavernous world where humans are content to live, far from the glimmer of Ideas. I will not decide one way or the other, I will push forward towards refusal. The sensible individual's disdain for politics lends a touch of irony to the description of the City of words, which, after all, is only conjured up in order to elucidate an *other* problem (the just and the unjust). In *The Republic* (putting aside *The Laws*), nothing is as it seems. The reflection on the inexistent, but possible City is not presented as a goal in itself. It is motivated by a negation of this particular *polis* and intermittently distances itself from all politics outside philosophical dialogue. It is as if this 'founding text' developed, according to an atopic irony, apolitical refusal *and*, despite everything, a return to an (ideal) order. As if Plato opened the way for apolitics without making a sacrifice to the one and only withdrawal. (Wouldn't we have a comparable ambiguity in Machiavelli's *The Prince*, both a handbook for managing the people and a steely exposition of the iniquity of politics?)

[3]

Under the distribution of governing realists, anything utopian today is qualified as *extremist*.[8] Correctly and incorrectly. An extremist speaks incessantly about the worst and the best, seen as if at the far ends of the real. Political extremism is a way of apprehending present and future horror as a threat in order to rally others around a radiant and other future. For this reason, we sometimes forget, there exists an extremism of the centre, one that could be represented by Solon stating that, without laws that take the middle ground, Athens would die,[9] or by a certain pro-European administrative propaganda (without the European Union, economic decline and world war would be certain). Political extremists, envisioning the limits of the practice of ordering in annihilation, acutely see the insurmountable incompetence [*impéritie*]. They designate an *extremity* to politics through which we could in fact exit. They are, therefore, more than other movements in the City, in part tied to the possibility of apolitics – even though the intensity of their engagement leads them at the same time to exaggerate their own refusal of refusal. On that point, political extremes thus 'meet' or 'come full circle', giving way to the pinnacle of totalitarianism and, by their very force, as soon as they overpower their adversaries. But they *designate* just as well, in their failure, the heterogeneous potentialities that they simultaneously impede and cultivate. The extremist 'no' registers an ambiguous promise, both fascinating and destructive. These elements of a praxis maintained within politics, which I am just beginning to touch on, don't have any more relevance than other elements. However, I suppose that their 'bad reputation' could play a part in a misplaced description of the apolitical gesture *via* militancy.

[4]

In this way *sabotage* harbours a negative force capable of bypassing partisan affiliations. The Marxist organisation of the workers' movement, in accord with the employers, isn't partial to Luddites because for the Marxists it is a question of *respecting* the means of production. With the relative waning of unionisation, and in situations of crisis where resignation is not enough, today's workers who are laid off from one day to the next may proceed to destroy in one form or another their former work tools. We're not faced with a regression – ah, the Communist vulgate … – but I fear that such behaviour has more to do with auto-liquidation than with an attitude of rebellion, following the example of those meltdowns where I kill my family and ten bystanders in the street before taking my own life. (These acts of murder, apparently more numerous and spontaneous in Northern societies, are the sterile episodes of rejecting the real, testifying to confusion between one's surroundings [*entourage*] and the world. The illusion is maintained through an increase in totalitarian control, making every parcel of common space the depository of the whole, and through a 'depoliticisation' that forces the *macro* onto the *micro*. As for the cause, it generally stems from a position of impotence trying to transform itself into one of omnipotence, with an arbitrary sampling of humans standing in for the whole.) It seems that today individual acting out in the form of random killing has replaced the threat of blowing up the factory.

Fierce opposition to the mill or textile manufacturing in England during the 1810s was not limited to backwardness or fear of 'Progress': it was more the becoming mechanical of the worker, liquidation of artisanal know-how, that had to be smashed to pieces. Derailing a train full of munitions is not *only* a struggle against the occupier, it also prevents murder and suspends the political direction of the act (in the French Resistance, objectives were not unified). Cracking a computer code and destroying police files attacks instruments of control without putting forth precise goals.

In sabotage, the lack of consequences serves as a means – as well as an impediment. This is because every act of sabotage may be recuperated and made to serve a political perspective; the greater the shift in political range (Resistance fighters, Luddites), the greater the inversion of political meaning (the hacker suddenly employed by a huge corporation or a state organisation to guard against others of his kind). A short circuit *occurs*, independently of the intentions and anterior or ulterior usages. In acts of sabotage, extremist militancy risks short-circuiting itself just as easily. We work our way in through cracks and gaps – beware of the bugs!

[5]

Obstruction or *blocking* is not just sabotage. Its ritualised form in the workers' movement is the strike, susceptible of being taken for an epic temporality, and almost always brought back down to ordinary protests making demands. The strike is the fear and the delight of trade unions, anxiety over the uncontrollable, and pleasure in winning at last, with everything put back in order through negotiations or political containment of the uprising. Too bad. Obstructing is a deictic refusal, one that could take aim at more than just material conditions, more than revolution, namely the *fact* of order. The limit, which it shares with sabotage, is in the delicate affirmation of an outside. The suspension of ordinary time in the clamour of the general assembly and the debates on the regeneration of the movement acquire for the participants an extra-political and surging value, one that bypasses the rancour of control. The May 1968 obstruction, in some of its legendary aspects, demonstrated an exteriority in festival [*la fête*], babble and neo-Romantic exaltation of love on the barricades. Unfortunately, in the end, it permanently retired such emancipatory themes as the foreshadowing of what comes after and rendered them, through indifference, subservient to a greater *political* urgency, one that would legitimate the uprising.

The Italian *operaismo* (or workerism) put obstruction at the centre of its revolutionary preoccupations, 'refusal of work' becoming in the writing of Negri 'both destruction of capital and auto-valorisation of class'.[10] Granting 'refusal' such an important role facilitated both an opening onto apolitics and its frenzied suppression since the imperative remained an alternative ordering of the same reality. In his 1966 work, Mario Tronti defines the two phases of the strategy of refusal: the first consists in

and, in the act, launched a series of regime changes in
frica, the Middle East and beyond. But is it anything
n a soldierly abolition? Under certain conditions, could
ion life being so degraded under the clutches of power
only way to make it liveable is to renounce it? I can't
r to avoid dogmatism. Suicide being less a short circuit
rmination, to consider the entirety of the event that it
es as (a refusal of) politics makes little sense. Early *nihil-*
ave striven for death by way of rupture. When Dimitri
v attempted tyrannicide in 1866, it seems that he
 the cost of his own life and by way of murder, to put on
e abysmal nothingness of power. In the instant he tried
ate the tsar, Karakozov could have been looking to
 the attraction of apolitics (rejection, interruption).[16]
 fact killed the emperor, thereby putting the *nothing*
e emptiness of absolute power, what outside would he
ed, but the prediction of his unliveable demise?
roadly, *abolition* is, at the very least, tied to the negativ-
efusal. Moments of ecstasy, the high points of pleasure,
 inscribed within the fabric of a regulated collective,
 often born of banned and authorised functions, are
n their experience as events, non-political. Georges
plored what these moments represent as accomplish-
cial configurations and a tearing away from the given.
al practice would amount to the unstable and recur-
t of 'expenditure', followed even into places hostile
dissolution that would endure after the flash, which
etuate into madness or the complete dissipation of all
d be the ambivalent example of a discursive sublime,
t of non-signification that apolitics would reach if we
itute it by way of destitution. I'm not so devout. The

'blocking the economic mechanism', and the second, 'political refusal'. It couldn't be any clearer: 'when we do manage to say "no", the refusal must make itself political, that is to say, active, which is to say, subjective, which is to say, organised'.[11] A normative and injunctive language is used in order to dissipate the possibility of a supplementary phase, that, of course, of apolitical refusal. It is symptomatic that the State becomes, in his writing, the almost exclusive bearer of a politics of domination. Negri writes about the 'totalitarian character' of reformism and denounces 'the manipulative function of the State at the borders of society',[12] all of which come together as an antipolitical description. However, in anchoring the critique in 'the State', obstruction becomes a transitory step whose 'experience' is erased. Revolutionary reflection in the end is satisfied with transposing an Italian social practice: the critique of politics limits itself to distrust of the central state; the refusal of work is obstinate inaction, literally doing nothing (*farniente*).

For Italian workerism work takes place in the factory, leaving the status of the production of thought completely undecided (does it require labour?). The driving force of *operaismo* came from academics, working to build up a doctrine, an activity that in itself was not meant to be blocked. Among Situationists, Debord took great pride in having 'invented' the slogan 'Never work' and in having put into practice a personal, wage-earner's refusal; in 1972, however, he railed against the so-called 'pro-situs' (pro-Situationists) for 'dread[ing] [...] work'.[13] In both cases, he presents 'work' as an absolute category, all the while referring back to a given type of activity, one that could be practical alienation, but that, in point of fact, is neither defined nor takes on specific qualities. This absence, in highly structured speeches, is symmetrical to the oblique and forbidden designation of apolitics. In this militant activity, at the very heart of political prose, could there be a surreptitious rupture with itself? At bottom, all of this 'in praise of laziness', following Paul Lafargue, Marx's cumbersome son-in-law, is a bizarre revolutionary tradition whose contradictions are not brought to greater heights by way of dialectics. Interrupting work is no idle task.

[6]

The fact that not one uprising since the end of the 1960s, in South America, Africa, Asia, Eastern Europe or the Middle-East has led to anything but ordinary representative regimes or revised dictatorships has left professional revolutionaries rather uncertain. The prestige of the *insurrection*, independently of what follows it, has only increased. There is a great temptation among 'radical' activists to treat these events with all too much credulity, while simultaneously redirecting them prophetically behind the scenes. An alliance persists, at the margins of the extreme left, of the 'commune' with the 'insurrection'[14] (an alliance that might conform to what Balibar names the 'structural ambiguity' of the 'very concept of politics' after 1789).[15] The latter assures the success of the former on a grand scale, which in the meantime serves as a point of retreat, a preparatory cell or laboratory of social experimentation. Revolutionary struggle is globally stuck in modes of action taken from the 1960s, including indigenism, guerrilla activity, terrorism, retreat into militant micro-ethics. In the duo commune-insurrection, exemplarily represented in France by the *Invisible Committee*, the jump between the two comes from a spatial delegation of tasks – communes in the villages, insurrections in the outskirts of the City [*banlieues*] – with 'blocking the economic mechanism', and the second, 'political refusal'. It couldn't be any clearer: 'when we do manage to say "no", the refusal must make itself political, that is to say, active, which is to say, subjective, which is to say, organised'.[11] A normative and injunctive language is used in order to dissipate the possibility of a supplementary phase, that, of course, of apolitical refusal. It is symptomatic that the State becomes, in his writing, the almost exclusive bearer of a politics of domination. Negri writes about the 'totalitarian character' of reformism and denounces 'the manipulative function of the State at the borders of society',[12] all of which come together as an antipolitical description. However, in anchoring the critique in 'the State', obstruction becomes a transitory step whose 'experience' is erased. Revolutionary reflection in the end is satisfied with transposing an Italian social practice: the critique of politics limits itself to distrust of the central state; the refusal of work is obstinate inaction, literally doing nothing (*farniente*).

For Italian workerism work takes place in the factory, leaving the status of the production of thought completely undecided (does it require labour?). The driving force of *operaismo* came from academics, working to build up a doctrine, an activity that in itself was not meant to be blocked. Among Situationists, Debord took great pride in having 'invented' the slogan 'Never work' and in having put into practice a personal, wage-earner's refusal; in 1972, however, he railed against the so-called 'pro-situs' (pro-Situationists) for 'dread[ing] [...] work'.[13] In both cases, he presents 'work' as an absolute category, all the while referring back to a given type of activity, one that could be practical alienation, but that, in point of fact, is neither defined nor takes on specific qualities. This absence, in highly structured speeches, is symmetrical to the oblique and forbidden designation of apolitics. In this militant activity, at the very heart of political prose, could there be a surreptitious rupture with itself? At bottom, all of this 'in praise of laziness', following Paul Lafargue, Marx's cumbersome son-in-law, is a bizarre revolutionary tradition whose contradictions are not brought to greater heights by way of dialectics. Interrupting work is no idle task.

[6]

The fact that not one uprising since the end of the 1960s, in South America, Africa, Asia, Eastern Europe or the Middle-East has led to anything but ordinary representative regimes or revised dictatorships has left professional revolutionaries rather uncertain. The prestige of the *insurrection*, independently of what follows it, has only increased. There is a great temptation among 'radical' activists to treat these events with all too much credulity, while simultaneously redirecting them prophetically behind the scenes. An alliance persists, at the margins of the extreme left, of the 'commune' with the 'insurrection'[14] (an alliance that might conform to what Balibar names the 'structural ambiguity' of the 'very concept of politics' after 1789).[15] The latter assures the success of the former on a grand scale, which in the meantime serves as a point of retreat, a preparatory cell or laboratory of social experimentation. Revolutionary struggle is globally stuck in modes of action taken from the 1960s, including indigenism, guerrilla activity, terrorism, retreat into militant micro-ethics. In the duo commune-insurrection, exemplarily represented in France by the *Invisible Committee*, the jump between the two comes from a spatial delegation of tasks – communes in the villages, insurrections in the outskirts of the City [*banlieues*] – with the hope of converging one day – in Paris, the capital city, naturally. *Both* the uprising *and* bar-grocery [*café-épicerie*] are deictic refusal *and* affirmation (even if only of chaos): they *evoke* apolitics, and *contain* it, quite literally. Insurrection turns to banditry or to a perpetually differed revolt, whether dystopic or utopic; the commune, despite its inevitable insertion, continues to dream of itself as anti-society, both eutopic and utopic. If something of the gratuitous violence of the insurrection, of its aptitude for disturbance pertains to apolitics, the flaw quickly falls prey to any parasitic movement, unless it firmly organises itself (and, by way of that, is lost). I would uphold the insurrection to live [*l'insurrection de vivre*], but on the condition that we situate the interruption there *in* the break.

[7]

The fact can't be denied or hidden that repeated uprisings, taken in their suspensive time, can drive a group to suicide, even to sacrifice, a tendency that proceeds perfectly from politics. The voluntary *martyr* constituted a theology of government for the first Christians, partisans of the liberation of colonised India, militants of Irish independence, soldiers of Al-Qaeda or ISIS – and all spring from a comparable faith: direct action, the superiority of Allah, the Emperor of Japan, or the civilising 'mission'. There exists an exteriority in dehiscence [*déhiscence*], that of the terrestrial or celestial paradise, in the 'future life' reserved for the brave or their descendants. However, sacrifice *totalises* equally, and no longer tolerates that an exit from life *could* be non-political.

I do not wish to downplay Mohamed Bouazizi's determination, the man who set himself on fire at the end of 2010 in

Tunisia and, in the act, launched a series of regime changes in North Africa, the Middle East and beyond. But is it anything more than a soldierly abolition? Under certain conditions, could we envision life being so degraded under the clutches of power that the only way to make it liveable is to renounce it? I can't say. Better to avoid dogmatism. Suicide being less a short circuit than a termination, to consider the entirety of the event that it constitutes as (a refusal of) politics makes little sense. Early *nihilism* may have striven for death by way of rupture. When Dimitri Karakozov attempted tyrannicide in 1866, it seems that he sought, at the cost of his own life and by way of murder, to put on display the abysmal nothingness of power. In the instant he tried to assassinate the tsar, Karakozov could have been looking to respond to the attraction of apolitics (rejection, interruption).[16] Had he in fact killed the emperor, thereby putting the *nothing* behind the emptiness of absolute power, what outside would he have attained, but the prediction of his unliveable demise?

More broadly, *abolition* is, at the very least, tied to the negativity of the refusal. Moments of ecstasy, the high points of pleasure, which are inscribed within the fabric of a regulated collective, which are often born of banned and authorised functions, are however, in their experience as events, non-political. Georges Bataille explored what these moments represent as accomplishments of social configurations and a tearing away from the given. An apolitical practice would amount to the unstable and recurring pursuit of 'expenditure', followed even into places hostile to it. The dissolution that would endure after the flash, which would perpetuate into madness or the complete dissipation of all force, would be the ambivalent example of a discursive sublime, or the point of non-signification that apolitics would reach if we tried to institute it by way of destitution. I'm not so devout. The vision of potlatch in *The Accursed Share* inscribes a social control of excess in rituals. Political canalisation of the transgressive is a cumbersome and perilous task for the City, it always risks getting out of hand – while, at the same time, it solidifies the ordinary (fools' day, carnival, Charivari, solar religion, Lupercalia). That meta-European societies today opt for a codified non-presence of transgression corresponds to the level of domination that has been attained, and can make them nostalgic for a different (and often fantastical) past. But the horde has already begun to order its disorder. Bataille, in *The Accursed Share*, *Inner Experience* and elsewhere, knew how to establish the relation between social limitation, rationalisation and politicisation. His outside, making use of literature and expenditure, takes on value today via its reconfiguration through experience. It would be a mistake to make of his work a simple breviary.

[8]

Universal extinction could strictly speaking be anti-political, because it would put an end to human order; this would be even more so polemically speaking (and thus militaro-politically as well). Rejecting the City, I say it again, does not mean trying to make it disappear *entirely*. Apolitics puts forward a singular mode of *living*, when *the* life of human animals is always already saturated with the necessity of social life. Politics precedes the refusal. 'Nuclear holocaust', an uninhabitable Earth are therefore not things to hope for, as long as we take an interest in the liveable. On the other hand, it is false to assert that the pillage and pollution of the planet are politically *senseless*. As unreasonable as it seems, the logic is easy. The ordering of order requires, as a final recourse, a risk of termination, the perspective of an end, which supremely justifies its existence. The positives: the 'kingdom of God' would descend upon the Earth, and, until then, we must give unto Caesar [*rendez-vous pour le reste à César*]. The negatives: if you are not on your best behaviour, beware of floods. Fear or expectation of divine intervention reinforces the acceptable reality of the organisation. The argument is not confined solely to the theologico-political; on the contrary, we find it everywhere. The *'grand soir'* (great night) of revolutionary upheaval is another way of legitimating politics (in relieving it of its present form), and so on. The 'unbelievable truth' of the contemporary population is the most egregious built-in threat, accomplished globally. On one hand, a nasty, destructive politics; on the other, a kind and protective politics; venomous states, rapacious multinationals, and vertiginous lands, green corporations; and both sides strongly agree, only the *polis* will decide. Look at the techno-democratic synthesis that is currently taking shape, with its experts, lawyers, engineers, zombie firms reincarnated. I don't want to mislead, I'm not denying the danger or the urgency. What I'm saying is that the devastation of the planet would rather sumptuously make politics indispensable, omnipresent, omnipotent, and all this regardless of 'bad' politics. The transfer of the sacred from churches to the world demands that the threat of an absolute end be ever more terrifying, concrete and global every time: the last hundred years have offered up global conflicts, generalised atomic explosion, the annihilation of the eco-system; the next great fear must reach the stars. All that is true, plausible. For a total regime, total destruction. Let us refuse the order of the order, rather than refute its wrongdoings or put hope in catastrophe and extinction. The political logic of annihilation is pragmatically implacable, right up to the untimely day when the horror becomes actual and total, by a sudden lack of control, which could happen.

The extremism of the refusal that I am articulating should not be confused with a politics of getting worse in order to get better. That form of politics, more modest in scope than the annihilation of the inhabitable world, currently amounts to dragging one's feet, and has few advantages. The extinction that might mildly titillate us would be more a form of non-procreation, which is effectively the best means to interrupt politics in its social preservation.

[9]

There are *forms of existence* that, representing the attempt at a continuing breakaway, cannot fully succeed, and veer at times towards caricature, at others towards opportunism. These *types* signal, however, an attempt at apolitics in that they designate possibilities. To typecast oneself into a role is erroneous, to figure oneself in a role not necessarily so. We can take on certain characters without becoming them.

Characters such as the 'rebel without a cause', a figure that asserted its importance gradually throughout the twentieth century. It is disparaged in direct proportion to the fascination it evokes. Nonetheless it harnesses a capacity of greater density in a rebellion that, without sacred or first cause, attacks the order of the order, flouts it furiously, sometimes idiotically, so much so that, on occasion, miraculously, yes, a refusal opens up, and, by way of it, attitudes that suspend the laws of the City. The expression 'rebel without a cause' seems to have spread in the United States largely due to the great outpouring of psycho-pathological criminology of the 1940s. First appearing as a title to a medical work in particular, it then spread further with the feature film by Nicolas Ray, *Rebel without a Cause* [whose French title translates back into English as *The Fury to Live*].[17] The main character, played by James Dean, is in the end no hero; in fact he proves himself rather inept, neither a thug nor a revolutionary. He balks, saying 'this can't be the future, this whole life is unliveable'. We can psychoanalyse him at our leisure, and, in the scene of the abandoned house, the fiction of a family uniting Jim, Judy and Plato (!) seems to stack the cards in favour of the logic of Oedipal overdetermination. Taking refuge in the non-place that is the observatory, opening onto the infinite of an inaccessible elsewhere and closing without *advancing* the plot from its point of departure, risks an escape route from all orderly societies, beyond construction of an alternative power (even if it were that of the band). The violence of the colours, the excess of play participate in this opening here, now, in a real that flouts the realism of social or aesthetic conventions. That, in any case, is what I find interesting in Ray's film, that all of this exists – even though nothing remains for too long. I understand the mockery against the juvenile delinquent, dumbfounded by his own future; I get the irritation at the unproductive squandering of forces and energy on an all too risky rebellion; I recognise the immediate degeneration of the glorious agitation into incivility that is all too convenient for the cops. To my mind what continues to draw us towards the figure of the rebel without a cause, beyond its limits and aberrations, its parody, its professionalisation, is that there remains in it a frenzied affirmation of another world, cut with intensities, affects, potent speech and forms.[18]

Adolescence raises fear. This 'age of life', based on specific biological changes, is in itself a social-historical construct. In the last couple of centuries of the so-called occidental world, and then extended globally, adolescence has become a temporal reserve much like other reserves, geographical ones, that enclose animals and wild humans. Categorisation of the adolescent through advertising, psychiatry, policing creates an *identity*, by definition *fleeting*, that distils the essential of the refusal. The advantage of such an identity is in bringing them back into the fold, already prophesied to infants by attentive parents; the risk for society would be to incite *every* adolescent to exit – out into the streets, further out of the City, and on to who knows where. Isn't this confirmed by the uprisings that are accumulating as I write these pages? Confining rebellion to a certain age veils the dangers to the established order. In parallel, everyone can see the efficacy of the ready-made story of collapse in the 'folly of youth'. This social script of adolescence casts political balking and, even more so, apolitical refusal as 'that which will pass'. If it must be, let us then be mature, belated adolescents.

[10]

The *hermit* is a type with a greater history. Whatever the reality of ecclesiastical dominations, the chance of no longer being assigned to only one discipline constructed 'in one body and one soul' is enough to motivate more than one sacred withdrawal. An itinerant Buddhist monk is not completely off the grid, and his subsistence depends on others giving alms. Similarly, the anchorite walled up in his cell, the Russian *poustinik* with ties to a village both receive charity from those around them. These positions conform to the cunning wisdom of traditional societies. The vagabond who goes from being 'without roof or law' to the French technocratic category for the homeless, *SDF* (*sans domicile fixe*), is nonetheless inventoried by default within a structure of social control. Thoreau, having retired to his cabin, still needed the help of his friend Emerson for laundry and a few meals. As for the hermits of Egypt, who followed St Anthony, they ended up bonding together to such a degree that, so the saying goes, 'the desert became a city of monks [...] who registered themselves for citizenship in Heaven'.[19]

Hermitage demonstrates that once the social fabric has taken form radical attempts at non-participation stabilise, up to a certain point. The difficulty comes from a retreat from the human collective – which encourages, by default, mysticism that steers towards a divine transcendence and the fusion with a world purported to be natural (Siddhartha, Francis of Assisi). The darkskinned slave, alone and wounded, the young unprepared ascetic going off 'into the wild' quickly destroy their lives, in the Antillean hills or the snows of Alaska. For Christopher McCandless, as for runaway blacks, the *ultra-individualist* route is not only a refusal of a particular placement on the grand chessboard, but more than that, it is a vibrant call for rupture. Death thus marks an incapacity to free oneself for good. Hermits save themselves from society in order to perish better; they endure so long as there is ritually organised charity, or they prepare monasteries. In the gallery of these ambiguous characters, Thoreau was right to give it a try, write a reflective account and then move on to other means.

[11]

The *dandy* is condemned by the ostentation of his exteriority to an interior exit. He is singled out by his clothes, mannerisms, pleasures, attitude. The *schools* of dandyism, punk *fashion* immediately efface a possible apolitics, converting it into trendiness and must-haves. Be that as it may, every time that I extravagantly indulge in the material composition of my existence, that I gesture towards excess, I question the particulars of the order. Think of African dandies [*la sape*],[20] think of Brummell, Baudelaire, Barbey. Dandies and other *phenomena* shed light on a marginal negativity to the text, which, at the risk of falling into insignificance or striking a pose of apolitical snobbery, offers up to the avid reader experiences at the extremities of the political body.

The *dog without a collar*, wandering without begging for anything more than odd scraps or, alternatively, making do with only what's under his roof (or in one's barrel for Diogenes), is the necessary counter-type to the dandy. Today, Diogenes would be thrown into an asylum just as dogs without collars rarely escape our contemporary kennels. In his grandiloquent fanaticism, Debord believed he could fashion himself as an itinerant and lofty dandy. Once the Situationist movement came to a close, he lived more than anything else off the return on his investments, playing and mastering his board game,[21] basking in the sun and sipping away leisurely. In short, he became the future 'national treasure'.[22] Debord demonstrates yet again the dangers of becoming established: even the marginal figure – in fact, especially the marginal – winds up only serving as decoration.

The *deserter* is the hero of the absence of heroism. In taking it upon oneself *not* to go to war, he or she demonstrates that, in the end, this 'no' can indeed be uttered, and that an exit from the field of battle is well within our reach. Without combatants, there would be no more war, and the militaro-political principle goes awry with this simple gesture, one word. That is what the deserter confides to us. He quite often pays for it with his life, the call for the liveable [*l'appel au vivable*] being worth very little to so many others. The other price for desertion is political reintegration (sometimes even for the mutineers themselves), and the armed man in the bush becomes a minister. The greatest incitement to jump ship, *Der Waldgang*, was written by Ernst Jünger, who, just a few years earlier, donned the German uniform in occupied Paris. It is not always easy to live up to one's own heights.

The evanescent merit of existing, that is what these examples of rebels, dogs, hermits, dandies, deserters and others demonstrate; an external affirmation by refusing politics. We should take guard against advances that are too unilateral, too permanent – to act more in the right is not to incarnate truth. I can make myself into this or that and then change back again. These figures of imposing stature are not my idols, rather they are signposts, already eroded, along the roads to explore. The different paths we may find ourselves treading weave together to form a labyrinth.

[12]

For apolitics, various experiments, perhaps shared among many, make a break and assert a beyond. That is why there is truly no apolitical *guide* – governing bodies, leaders, *duces* and *führers* are not for us but for others [*les autres*]. We have to make do with anthologies, a trove of curiosities, collected essays; and we must retrace each of their singular courses as we put them to the test [*À chaque singularité revient d'éprouver des parcours*].

In a regime of absolute destruction and constraint, if an exit is still possible, it is all the more difficult and all the more costly. I am consistently motivated by an attempt to undo the totalitarian hold. That is accomplished every day by those of us who break ranks; it is *also* assured by engagement in the service of disengagement. There is no apolitical programme to articulate, nor is there truly a politics to apolitics. As in the examples of discontent and protest, which are redirected by the *polis* for its own benefit, some political formations are subject to erosion. In conducting singular experiments, liberating ourselves from liberation, I believe all the more in certain promises of art and thought, in our compound faculties, our feelings and in action taken to its maximum. But it would be strange to meticulously delve into apolitics without taking into account deviation or perversion of the ordinary. I am not urging anyone to throw themselves as the proverbial spanner in the works, to join a cell or to take hold of a megaphone. It is not a question of returning for the nth time to a known dialectic; we would do better to speak of a doubling of the real.

[13]

In apolitical matters, it is best not to expect much from the community or communities and to be wary of passing from forms of existence to *clubs* – however theoretically sophisticated or *negative* they might be. The old Aristotelian category of 'community' did not restore the collective back to an archi-concept, and did not unambiguously yoke distinct assemblages to the *polis*. 'All communities appear as political parties', assures the *Nicomachean Ethics*. The claim, in all its nudity, still strikes me as valid, and I would eagerly invite proponents of communities to explain in what way their practices could in some sense disturb the very ordering of order. Communitarianism may be able to upset the domination of parties [*le règne des partis*] in the State, but, in its place, it establishes the rule of holistic parts [*la règle des parties*] and compassionately maintains the organised body.

After the disappointment of the *communes* of the 1960s and 1970s, a large philosophical effort was made to situate *the* community, apart from the ancient *polis*. A lot could be said about this effort, and I responded to this debate myself in *À force d'amitié*, which I will touch on briefly here. Certainly, Giorgio Agamben, Jacques Rancière and Jean-Luc Nancy attempted to restore 'the' community that could serve as a refuge where forms of existence bordering on anti-political could come together. However, for these authors, it is only ever a question of *rebuilding* a new *polis*. Under the name 'the coming community', Agamben identifies the 'novelty of the coming politics'.[23] The 'community of speaking beings', the 'community of sharing'[24] come together in the 'egalitarian event'[25] that could be May 1968, or even the French Revolution or literary democracy. Nancy, while challenging the idea that an 'inoperative community' could serve as a foundation to 'a' politics,[26] seeks to uncover 'the' political[27] in the ordering of community as such. A massive problem comes along with this, however, that essentially subordinates, almost systematically, elective affinities and the shifting fragility of affect to the functioning of 'the' community between subjects, which then takes precedence over and predetermines their relations. And, as if by chance, he has made precious little place for friendship among the advocates of the community (with the notable, although complicated, exception of Maurice Blanchot).[28]

What is at stake for us is not rediscovering the communal (biological or cultural), nor forging a communality by way of the symbolic, nor building a community or communities. Rather, we're striving to open up and explore a space that could be shared by us.[29]

[14]

If I wanted to politically combat politics (to stop at that, believe me, would entrap us; and to completely turn away from it, I fear, would leave us even more precariously alive), this is what I would do: I would work to reduce institutional organisations, I would fight for the emergence of something else, I would denounce the powers that be, my actions would criticise conformity. Every position has its risks – let us not take anything as definitive, let us nonetheless try to say more.

We are the ones who make instituted organisations and participate in them, well then, let us be the ones who curtail them. Let us stop them from proliferating if they serve little purpose. *Reduction* doesn't have to lead us to belief in destruction. I distrust systems of compensation. Libertarians, fringe of the American right – individualist, unabashedly hedonistic and what the French would call 'ultra-liberal' – represent the old tradition in the United States of a struggle for small government; and, in the end, they transfer powers of the 'public' to the 'private', as can be seen even in a sophisticated thinker such as Robert Nozick.[30] A multinational is no less organised, no less instituted than a state. I don't have any more sympathy for militias than for the police. As to the 'free' market ... In other words, reducing institutions requires that we first understand the extent of social organisation (something the libertarians don't get). Limiting the role of governments is associated with a critique of a centre of national or federal command that takes hold of every aspect of existence, and, in that way, paves the way for an apolitical refusal. But it only amounts to yet another ordinary, insidious effacement of apolitics, when it allows the capitalist enterprise to commission the organisation of vital forces for its own ends. In the United States, it is the sordid alternative between health control by a governmental consortium – and its management by private insurance companies.

Reduction – being carried out not to the detriment of the collective, rather, inversely, against totalitarianism – asserts itself as a gesture of cohesion. It takes on meaning both outside a slogan that would reduce all organisations to the same level and beyond localised dogma (anti-state or pro-movement, anti-party or pro-civil society, anti-union or pro-general assembly, and so on). Yes, but what meaning? The withdrawal, the lack of politicisation, acted out in the hiatus of social order. The active 'critique' of power and conformism are correlated. It implicates each and every political dimension that I have touched on, attacking hierarchical principles, effects of authority, modes of existence and what governance takes as given. Power, in itself, is neither *evil* nor *bad*. It can be *criticised*, and the domination that it produces and legitimates can be contested. The *emergence* of something else is what follows. Emergence, or revolution? So long as we bear in mind that in the aftermath *it* will continue, differently ... The emergence of something else, which stands in the way, which clears the way [*qui contrecarre et qui ouvre*]; it is worthwhile to go along with it, encourage it, defend it before the predictable hardens into an inflexible reality [*avant la prévisible pose du ciment*].

[15]

It seems to me that reduction, emergence, denunciation, critique form an extension of politics that proves to be *less* adverse to its own refusal than other totalitarian formations. It goes without saying, however, that no *organisation* readily paves the way for its own negation. Calculation encourages power to mask its exercise here and there in order to avoid the consequences of an exaggerated invasion – even though cybernetics can make miracles happen. Politicised resistance is a better guarantor, one that, once again, runs the risk of erasing, proportional to its own success, an even greater refusal. A certain leftism, one which disdains organisations, limits itself to the dimensions I've indicated (most of the time – it willingly forgets half of it); we can find good material there for a comedy or even a drama once the philosopher-writer crowns himself king. The same goes, even worse, for every activist who would double as an apolitician [*Il en va de même, et en pis, pour tout activiste qui se doublerait d'un apolitique*]. I was very entertained by my own actions at a time when, before being won over by the truth of the party, I also tried to convince professional militants of this other of the other. Ah! Why not come take up residency in the royal suite of the *Grand Hotel Abyss* instead of settling down at *The International*?[31] If, from the point of view of right-minded people, political refusal, and above all the extreme left, is irresponsible and grotesque, apolitics is a farce for everyone. Yes, why not laugh about it as well? Satire often harbours more than just clownishness. Transgressive characters among marionettes (the Turkish Karagöz, the Punch and Judy show at the time of the Lyon silk workers, Jarry's *Père Ubu*) manage to *show* that the powerful are puppets, that their strength rests on emptiness and violence. This anti-political *representation* also affirms; the small puppet theatre, the screen for shadow puppets only afford a very minor relief; laughter as a way out, that is the essential. Mockery that goes well beyond simple parody *aimed* at someone or something projects us into a liveable state, one that is sometimes the best resource for those far removed from the seats of power. I invite you to join me; let us laugh and laugh to the point where the orderly motivation of derision echoes the ineffable capers of authoritarian society, which is held up only by its own fiction despite its haughty airs of importance.

[16]

Hysterical laughter [*le fou rire*] doesn't sit well with the militaro-political. It's true that we don't refuse that way [*on refuse autrement*] – or that the farce comes to an end one day. Are we then in anarchism if we struggle to build an elsewhere *here and now* by way of a break, while at the same time adopting a few extreme gestures and rejecting the laws of the clan? Anarchism is so multiform, I don't expect anything special from its majority incarnations. The circle in which the A of *Anarchism* is inscribed in its well-known graffiti sign is certainly an O, graphically presenting the affirmation, 'anarchy is order' [*l'anarchie c'est l'ordre*].[32] It's useless to add to this new catechism of political alpha and omega: this is certainly not my line of thought. The religion of repealable mandates (where the people could revoke their electors), common to both anarchos and Bolsheviks, is an interesting *power* technique; by making itself into a command, it remains the prop of chieftains. I have more sympathy for a strain of anarchism articulated most prominently by Émile Armand. From the start of the 1900s, he called for a change in behaviour and a 'presentist' insurrection of desire, both allied to a virulent critique of social and political constructions.[33] So far, so good. But (like with Stirner) I have trouble with his credo of 'by and for the individual',[34] who 'wants to live his life [...] without having to think about the rest of the world'. What are we to make of this vision of the self, this 'ego', who strives 'to maintain a "mastery of self"', who considers its faculties 'as so many servants',[35] and who often seems subservient to its own demand for freedom ('live *freely*, live your own personal conception of life')?[36] The subject, ego, self, person, subjectivity – at whatever level they operate, either as one or more or less than that – are psychological and metaphysical instances with indistinct contours and highly politicisable contents. The 'individual' is an appellation that grows out of an affective and cognitive impression of 'being by difference', as it refers to itself in the counting of bodies. It is a common mechanism of control to define this impression *by* numbering it (the prisoner becomes a number[37]), thereby trying to minimise it (the *emptiness* of hearts and minds in Taoism[38]), or even to destroy it. In reaction, a certain *an*archism can then take up the cause and fight for the *individual*. I share in the energy of denial and scandal; the mistake would be then to put one's trust in individual form as in a deity. Marx and Engels were right to emphasise that attachment to the 'properties' of the 'ego', in Stirner for example, was not independent of the structures of capitalist society: the safeguard of one's little self, the passion for its own rules, in fact comes under a 'governance' of the 'ego' that is open to all modes of political surveillance. Of course, Marx and Engels take the individual as a bodily, biological unit that produces its 'means of living'; in making 'consciousness [...] a social product',[39] they proceed to close and lock securely all the gates to the City, with us inside.

I tend to think that only singularities – neither pre-individual, archi-unitary nor *given* once and for all – are capable of living *apolitics*.[40] In the violent tearing asunder of the self, constituted such that it may send forth an 'I', in the brief production of a shared experience (and not a *common* or *communal* one), in the creation of a fissure to pass through, we are far removed from individualism and close to a deictic refusal. No need to demand the inalienable rights of the person, to strive to protect the integrity of the subject, in order to cultivate apolitics.[41] It is enough to access just once some life outside of the ordinary [*de la vie autre*] to be immediately sensitive to encouraging its event.

To return to Émile Armand, I hardly see the point in supporting an intensely political category (anarchism) if it is a question of using this name to designate an exit from the old fortress of the City. As much as I like the portrait of the anarchist 'as asocial, disobedient, unadapted, an outsider, someone on the margins or sidelines',[42] these characteristics are insufficient for the supplementary step, beyond any discussion of the 'struggle for existence'. Now, it should be clear, I have no dog in that fight. Armand is such an eccentric figure that I would like to see myself in *his* definition of the anarchist, if such a thing is necessary. Is it necessary? For whom? For what? In the service of what memories, to attend to what organisations, what systems of visibility?

[17]

Excerpts for *New Reflections of an Apolitical Man* [*Nouvelles considérations d'un apolitique*].[43]

First part (November 2010). 'I have no lessons to give. What a relief. I turned thirty-seven last week, I don't quite know what that means. I am in places, social settings, geographies, politics I was not meant for. Despite the malaise, sorrows, I continue to believe that this existence that I have made for myself, or that has made me, is alive, and liveable, more, I venture to say, than many ... Very young, I was fascinated by the *guignol politique*, on this I had no revelations of grandeur.

'... At first, I didn't like school. The phonies on the playground bothered me even more than the old republican discipline, its hygiene-ism, its conformism. However, I had no nostalgia for any "natural environment", so, well ... I made the choice of no fixed choices in love. It was decided for me straight away, I only talked about it some time later. I had a desire for revolution, nourished by more or less easy transgression ... I was the type of student for whom the movement meant something, in protests, in occupying; and who, the evening of the march and at night, would return to philosophy, poetry – or would replay its passion for myself ... On more than one occasion I gave in, to make up for something ... I kept up my engagement, I briefly drew a salary from inept consulting, all the while talking about the temptation of *suave mari magno* in the face of the disaster that is the world. Following some audacious choices here and there, a few machinations and some serious misunderstandings, I left legally for the United States, where my improbable condition as "private thinker"[44] under contract leaves me with plenty of time and books in order to write and corrupt youth, doling out in three weeks the equivalent of what I earned in a year of hard times in Paris; how unfortunate, then, that for all that one has to put on a perennial smile, accept to be a university trinket and find oneself in the thick of democratic totalitarianism; but what a slow death for France, and all that comes with it ... Furthermore, upper management ... had no idea what I was developing; except when it happened ... an *ad personam* attack: your argument is very elegant, but what sort of behaviour does it support? In truth, I don't know ... Where does all of this lead us? *Nowhere fast?* ... Please exploit this as much as you will [*Que l'on se serve sur la bête, et du présent paragraphe*] ...'

Second part (April 1998–May 2002). 'I resent that she doesn't understand that the revolution includes the antisociety of friends; she doesn't put enough stock into it. The equalisable – importation of the structure of equalisation – commerce – politics ... I want to side with life in as much as it is life – life in rupture, fragile and liveable life ... There is a political urgency, an urgency of politics ... Politics must abandon any and all pretension to stability, be it of historical facts or philosophical concepts ... Wherever the organisation of a party, of a class-based labour union takes after company organisation, failure. Does one ever leave prison alive? ... *Because we must make this life liveable* ... Can we make distinctions in life? untangle life [*la vie*] (or *a* life or *one's* life or ...) from some living [*de la vie*]? Can we avoid doing such things? And in either case how or what will we live if ever they are distinct? ... To cite Deleuze, I'd like to believe in a "revolutionary-becoming of people" [*devenir-révolutionnaire des gens*];[45] but I wonder how it could come into contact with the becoming-revolutionary of politics without it being overwhelmed, torn apart, domesticated: ... a *skēpsis tōn politikōn* ... an anti-political politics?'

Everything must begin anew, always.

[18]

Alongside political posters and daily newspapers, let us also post bills and publish journals of apolitics. Blogs, which ordinarily enable the triumph of an inane expressivity, could be useful for once, and become the discontinuous annals of episodic refusals.

'We have just completed our thirteen thousand five hundredth day of not driving. It was nothing extraordinary, let's make no mistake. Nonetheless, by abstaining from this mobile commodity for individuals, we caused some disturbance. How many times have we been ridiculed: no sensible person would deprive herself of the cherished set of wheels. And even more intolerable to the voice of social reason, our indifference to the justification: not a long explication on capitalist development or pollution (if it was not known at the time, then later), no childhood trauma where the family perishes in an accident, we just don't like it and that's that. During this time when everyone made counteraccusations, we saw other birds at the tops of trees, we went over the suspension bridge, strange people spoke to us in the night of cities. – I already regret having confessed it, in the end I am but one among many, but, well, over and above the constant humiliation of being a foreigner, I take joy, light but firm, in remaining a metic. – The social fabric is destroyed in the improbable instant when, by way of so many artifices, and through protective windows, despite everything, I exchange looks and words with an ape. Everything in this laboratory is political, every person has been implicated in a complex game of incessant power relations, and the experience itself follows directly from the Aristotelian definition. There I am with a non-human animal (*zoōn*) that has language (*logon ekhon*). As we play together, with one word, he points spontaneously to these *masks* being used to hide our faces. There is suddenly nothing more than the flash of an exchange with another animal that has been excluded in advance. We are *together* a thousand miles from all the places of the *polis*. – You have to give yourself a certain body type – the one, toned, that you get through the equipped discipline of gyms, or the other, the double result of addiction to synthetic sugars and of the immobility of the spectator to one's existence: ah, surely no. – She wanted neither to marry, adopt nor procreate, she had thought about renouncing her citizenship, then learned that she would never be stateless, and gave it up. – Our group, we would sometimes see each other morning and night, talking for hours, throw ourselves into reciprocal imitation, still laugh about the friend who fell asleep in the middle of a sentence during the course of a meal. And this guy with whom we *work*, for the same journal, who lectures me, 'whatever you say, we are a po-li-ti-cal body'. Yes, yes, for you, yes, sure, we are nothing but that. – The music stops, we hear nothing but the creaking of the masts in the wind, the image is going to disappear, what to do?

In what Joyce named *epiphanies*, there one can find the seeds of apolitics. Let us also see that this collection of essays, that has a thousand ramifications more elaborated in the chronicles of its creation, is not just a *catalogue* or an *inventory*. It is up to us to *activate* these instances – not act them out, act on them, shake them up; nor exactly to reactivate, overactivate or actualise them.

[19]. Coda

A way to access the non-political real is through the obstinacy of the refusal, through affirmation, together. This *apolitics* is woven throughout literature, arts, sentiment, research, bodily practices, sharing, ecstasy, laughing, speech, excess, extremism, forms of life – without ever automatically guaranteeing effects and without being co-opted ordinarily. These are only fits and starts. To recognise the vital importance of these experiences, including what limits them, was the goal of this introduction, because what I am pursuing, more than necessary critique, is that the rest remains to be written in multiple ways in our stories, histories, adventures and treatises, by all of those who make us who we are. Such an attempt runs the risk of occultation, caricature: we're not going to stop for something so minor …

Since apolitics exists by flashes, we will inevitably fall back down. I have cultivated different arts of fleeing for so long that I wouldn't know how to count them; and nevertheless I live in this world. Sustainable disdain for all politics taken to its limits, right up to withdrawal into the infinite landscape, the jungle, study, the urban desert or even hermitage. We have to take heed, especially in this totalitarian state of the world, that the complete lack of concern for society does not give rise to ignorance of the diffuse, with politics treated as contraband. Furthermore, if we were to turn refusal of order into the order of the day, which would hold others back, wouldn't we have gone completely astray? (Please do not fear devilish contradictions; after all, we are not after any unity of combat.) I hardly see how an insistent militancy (for the proletariat, identity, markets, pure knowledge, the living, animal rights, aestheticism and so on) could avoid trying to rebuild an ordering of order, regardless of any gaps in extremism. As for political action, it is not destroyed by apolitics; rather, it is momentarily ruined. It is a dangerous game to wash one's hands of everything; a perilous one to use partisan means to achieve what they elide; and, finally, a risky one to hazard partitioning oneself in order to work in opposing directions; nothing holds any more, play your hand.

This book does not speak in your name, it hardly responds to mine. It speaks to us. It is a voice, voices, paths. It may be a virus.

[20]

During the recent protests in Greece, a sign appeared, one, it seems, that spread from wall to wall with minor variations. The more sombre saw in it the dissemination of a logo, perhaps a visual branding of a group whose identity had yet to come, a few lines that meant nothing, but signalled. Shouldn't we rather read the irregular figure as a '*sampi*', an archaic character, whose form varied greatly in the old Ionia of Byzantium? *Sampi* coded *900*, thus just prior to the magic *thousand*, and could designate a multitude on the verge of affirming itself, the revolt that precedes the revolution. Unless it is a '*pi*' crossed out, the *p* of politics, the *polis*, written, initialised, then crossed out, overtaken, outstripped, left behind – like a difference over its ordinary sign ($\neq$). Not a sign of propaganda, the mark of a provocation?

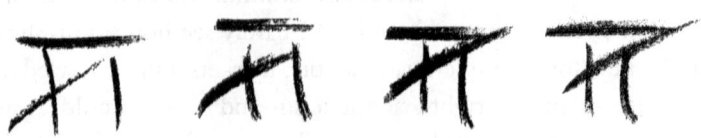

Notes

1 Michel Foucault, *Le Corps utopique: suivi de Les hétérotopies* (Paris: Lignes, 2009 [1966]).
2 The Invisible Committee, *The Coming Insurrection* (Los Angeles: Semiotext(e), 2009).
3 The alter-globalisation movement [*altermondialistes*] sought above all to establish a world *other* [*autre*] (and 'better'). However, I wouldn't rely too much on them if the question is truly of an *other* possible world [*un* autre *monde possible*].
4 Plato, *The Republic*, trans. Allan Bloom (New York: Basic Books, 1991), IX.592a, p. 274.
5 Ibid., VII.540d, p. 220.
6 Ibid., IX.591c. (translation modified). Bloom translates it as 'the man who has intelligence', p. 274.
7 See Leo Strauss, *Persecution and the Art of Writing* (Glencoe: Free Press, 1952).
8 Here I am expanding on a reflection on extremism that I began in 'Chroniques de la fin du monde', *Labyrinthe*, 19:3, 2004, pp. 31–42.
9 Solon, *Poetarum Elegiacorum Testimonia et Fragmenta*, trans. B. Gentili and C. Prato (Leipzig: Teubner, 1988), fr. 3.
10 Antonio Negri, *Il Dominio e il sabottaggio: Sul Metodo Marxista della Transformazione Sociale* (Milano: Feltrinelli, 1979), p. 46.
11 Mario Tronti, *Operai e capitale* (Turin: Einaudi, 1966), pp. 250ff.
12 Antonio Negri, *Proletari e Stato* (Milan: Feltrinelli, 1979), p. 32.
13 Guy Debord, *The Real Split in the International: Theses on the Situationist International and Its Time, 1972*, trans. John McHale (London: Pluto Press, 2003), § 28, p. 35.
14 See The Invisible Committee, *The Coming Insurrection*, especially pp. 101ff, 117ff, 135.
15 Etienne Balibar, *Les Frontières de la démocratie* (Paris: La Découverte, 1992), p. 139.
16 See Claudia Verhoeven, *The Odd Man Karakozov: Imperial Russia, Modernity, and the Birth of Terrorism* (Ithaca, NY: Cornell University Press, 2009).
17 *Rebel Without a Cause*, film, directed by Robert Mitchell Lindner, USA: Warner Bros, 1944.
18 I also take up the French verlan '*bel-re*' in 'Le Rénégat', *Labyrinthe*, 32, 2008, pp. 55–7. See also Michel Onfray, *Politique du rebelle: Traité de Résistance et d'Insoumission* (Paris: B. Grasset, 1997) and, in a very different

Index

Abbé Sieyès, 7
adolescence, 90–1
Adorno, Theodor, 59–61
Aeschylus, 36
aestheticism, 45–6, 107
Agamben, Giorgio
  biopower, biopolitics, 9
  community, 96
  state of exception, 29
Algeria, 77, 49n
anarchism, 11
  Émile Armand, 100–2
  encore un effort!, 69
  individualism, 101
animals, 7, 46, 53, 55, 87, 91
  formation of the social, 14
  language, 105–6
  rights, 107
anti-politics, 1, 4, 42, 44, 59–60, 87, 96, 100, 104; *see also* non-political, the; apolitics
apolitics, 4, 11, 12–13, 16–18, 21–5, 30, 41–5, 54, 60, 62, 64, 68, 70, 75, 79, 82, 84–9, 93, 94, 95, 98, 99, 103–8
  non-political, relation to the, 70–1
  singularities, relation to, 102
  see also anti-politics; politics
Arab Spring, 3
  Bouazizi, Mohamed, 85

architecture
  Le Corbusier, 61–2
  Michelangelo, 62
  Thoreau, Henry David, 62
  Turrell, James, 62
  Van der Rohe, Mies, 62
  Vauban, Sebastien Le Prestre de, 61–2
Aristotle, 105
  animals, 28
  bios and *zōē*, 40
  community, 95–6
  ethics and politics, 39–41
  exit from politics, 39–40
  friendship, 40
  regimes, 38
art, 59–63, 68, 70, 95, 107
  l'art pour l'art, 59
  revolution, relation to, 63–4
  see also architecture; literature; Situationism
atopia, 5
Aurelius, Marcus, 23
auto-(or self-)organisation, 3

Babeuf, Gracchus, 30
Badiou, Alain, 12
  apolitics, the apolitical, 12
  biopolitics, 12
  event, 12

INDEX

'politics of non-domination', 13
'pre-political', 13
Rancière, critique of, 12, 23–4
Balibar, Etienne, 84
Bataille, Georges, 86–7
biopolitics, 9–10, 12
bio-zoopolitics, 53
biopower, 9
bios and *zōē*, 10, 40, 47n
Blanqui, Louis Auguste, 69
Bouazizi, Mohamed, 85
Brazil, 3
Breton, André, 56
Burnham, James, 32
Butler, Judith, 20

Cacciari, Massimo, 41–2
capitalism, 31, 35, 37, 38, 55, 68, 82, 98, 101, 105
Castoriadis, Cornelius, 28
Césaire, Suzanne, 20
China, 3, 35
Cold War, 21
colonialism, 18, 29, 77
communism, 22, 40, 45, 55, 80
Communitarianism, 96
concentrated, 17, 19–21, 27, 29, 31, 38, 48n, 69
 diffuse, distinction between, 17
 see also diffuse
Confucius, 17
Coupat, Julien, 23

Dada, 63–4
dandy, 93–4
Debord, Guy
 art and life, 65
 as dandy, 93
 on work, 83
 see also Situationism; spectacle
Deleuze, Gilles
 'private thinker', 103
 'revolutionary-becoming of people' [*devenir-révolutionnaire des gens*], 104

Derrida, Jacques
 friendship, 24
 'to-come' vs *Realpolitik*, 9–10
 deserter, 93–4
 Der Waldgang by Ernst Jünger, 94
Dieudonné, 4
differance, 10
diffuse, 8, 17, 19–21, 27, 28, 48n, 69, 107
 concentrated, distinction between, 17
 see also concentrated
Diogenes, 93
discourse [*parole*], 9; *see also* speech [*parole*]
distraction, 34
'dog without a collar', 93
drug use, 61
 apolitics, relation to, 70
Dubreuil, Laurent
 À force *d'amitié*, 5, 49n, 72n, 96, 110n
 Empire of Language, 5, 47n, 48n
 Intellective Space, 49n
 Pures fictions, 50n

ecstasy, 36, 61, 86, 107
Engels, Friedrich *see* Marx, Karl
Epictetus, 23
Esposito, Roberto, 9
 impolitico, 41–2
European Union, 31, 79
 European Bank, 3

Fanon, Frantz, 18
fascism, 21, 29, 39
feminism, 18–19
Fordism, 32
Foucault, Michel, 23
 'heterotopias', 76
Fourier, Joseph, 76
France, 3, 4, 22, 84–5, 92
 'mediatised parliamentary democracy', 38

113

school and university system, 103–4
Socialist Party, 55
zadistes, 4
see also French Resistance
Frankfurt School, 22
French Resistance, 81

Gentile, Giovanni, 21–2
Greece, 3
recent protests, 108
Grillo, Beppe, 4

Hanisch, Carol, 19
Hardt, Michael and Antonio Negri, multitude, 9–10
hermit, 91–2, 94, 107
Hessel, Stéphane, 2
Hong Kong, 3
Hugo, Victor, 58

impolitical [*impolitico*], 41
inconstructible, the, 3, 26, 32, 49n
indigenismo, 19–20, 84
  zadistes, neo-indigenist movement, 4
indignados, 1
indiscipline, 44, 52n
insurrection, 2, 4, 7, 23, 64, 84–5, 101
  'the coming insurrection' [*l'insurrection qui vient*], 77
Internationale, The, 7
internet, 4, 30–1, 34, 35
Invisible Committee, the [*le Comité Invisible*], 84–5
Italy, 4, 41, 76, 82–3

Jarry, Alfred, 100
Joyce, James, 106
Jullien, François, 42–3
Jünger, Enrst, 21–2, 94

Kacem, Mehdi Belhaj, 38
Kampf, 35
Kant, Immanuel, 58

Karakozov, Dimitri, 86
Khmer Rouge, 17
Ku Klux Klan, 17

Laclau, Ernesto and Chantal Mouffe, 24
Lafargue, Paul, 84
laughter, 99–100, 106, 107
  hysterical laughter [*le fou rire*], 100
Leninism, 29
liberal democracy, 21
libertarians, 97
life/some life [*la vie/de la vie*], 47n, 54–5, 61, 72n, 102, 104
  art, relation to, 61
literature, 57–60, 87, 107
  anti-politics, relation to, 59–60
  art, relation to, 60–1
  ivory tower, 58, 107
  parlance, relation to, 57
  political order, relation to, 57–8
  politicisation, 58–9
live well [*bien vivre*], 2
Loraux, Nicole, 59
Luddites, 80–1
Lysenko, Trofim, 26

McCandless, Christopher, 92
Machiavelli, Niccolò, 79
mafia, 17
Marcuse, Herbert
  art and revolution, 63
  technology, 33
macro-politics, 17–19, 32, 80; see also micro-politics; politics
Maoism, 21
Marx, Karl, 84; see also Marx, Karl and Friedrich Engels
Marx, Karl and Friedrich Engels, 56
  The German Ideology, 37
  individual, on the, 101–2
Marxism, 3, 35, 37, 56, 80
  formal democracy, 31
May 1968, 23, 64, 82, 96

INDEX

media, 8, 18, 30–1, 33, 38
  facebook, 4
  liberty of the press, 30
  twitter, 4
  see also technology
Meillassoux, Quentin, 43
Meschonnic, Henri, 58
micro-politics, 17–19, 32, 80; *see also* macro-politics; politics
Milner, Jean-Claude, 9
molar level, 17, 21, 48n, 76; *see also* molecular level
molecular level, 8, 15, 17–19, 21, 38, 48n, 76; *see also* molar level
More, Thomas, 75–6
Moreiras, Alberto
  anti-politics, 42
  intrapolitics vs imperial politics, 9
Mouffe, Chantal, 25
  politics 'to-come' vs *Realpolitik*, 9–10
  see also Laclau, Ernesto and Chantal Mouffe

Nancy, Jean-Luc
  community and *polis*, 96–7
  community of the political vs communal politics, 9
  non-political, the, 25
Nazism, 17, 21, 29, 32, 35
Negri, Antonio, *operaismo* (workerism), 82–3; *see also* Hardt, Michael and Antonio Negri
non-political, the, 4, 15, 25–9, 36, 41, 44–5, 85, 86, 107
  anti-politics, relation to, 60
  apolitics, relation to, 70
  inconstructible, the, 26–7
  see also anti-politics; the political [*le politique*]

obstruction or blocking, 82–3
operaismo (workerism), 82–3
strike, 82

Occupy movement, 1
  technology, 34
  'we are the 99%', 4
October 1961, events of, 23, 49n

parlance [*parlure*], 4, 16, 18, 33, 47n, 57; *see also* discourse [*parole*]; phrase; phraseology; speech [*parole*]
Pascal, Blaise, 33
phrase, 24, 30, 32, 48n, 57, 68; *see also* phraseology
phraseology, 18, 21, 48n; *see also* phrase
Plato, 40, 77–9, 90
the political [*le politique*], 8, 9, 10, 12, 19, 20, 25, 34, 35, 40, 41, 42, 46, 46n, 64, 96
  economy, relation to the, 37–8
  juridical-political, the, 35–6
  militaro-political, the, 35–7, 44, 87, 100
  politics, disctinction between, 15
  theologico-political, the, 35–6, 59, 88
  see also non-political, the; politics [*la politique*]
politics [*la politique*]
  ability to change life [*changer la vie*], 55–7
  identity, relation to, 19–20, 67–8, 91, 107
  political, distinction between the, 15
  spectacle, relation to, 48n
  subject, the, 19, 33
  technology, relation to, 35–7
  see also anti-politics; apolitics; impolitical [*impolitico*]; macro-politics; micro-politics; non-political, the; political, the; spectacle
Popper, Karl, 22
private vs public, 19, 39
'private thinker', 103–4

INDEX

queer, 19–20

Rancière, Jacques
  Badiou's critique of, 12
  community and *polis*, 96
  Disagreement, 23–4
  literature, 58–9, 96
  On the Shores of Politics, 23–4
  police, 9–10, 24
  politics vs police, 9–10
Rawls, John, 16
'rebel without a cause', 89–90
  film by Nicholas Ray, 90
revolution, 58, 59, 62–4, 66, 76–7, 82–4, 88, 90, 98, 103, 104, 108
  French Revolution, 102
  professional revolutionary, 84
  'revolutionary-becoming of people' [*devenir-révolutionnaire des gens*], 104
Rimbaud, Arthur, 56
Rizzi, Bruno, 32

sabotage, 80–2
sacrifice, 85
  Bouazizi, Mohamed, 85
Saint Anthony, 92
Saint-Simonians, 77
Sainte-Beuve, Charles Augustin, 58
sampi, 108
Sartre, Jean-Paul, 59
Schmitt, Carl
  The Concept of the Political, 35
  militaro-political, 35
Sieyès, Emmanuel Joseph, 7
Situationism, 63–5, 83, 93
  relation to Dada and surrealism, 63–4
  spectacle, the, 64
  see also Debord, Guy; Vaneigem, Raoul
Sloterdijk, Peter, 43

Solon, 53–4, 79
sovietism, 21
spectacle, 3, 8, 21, 29, 62, 64
  Society of the Spectacle, 48n
  see also Debord, Guy; Situationism
speech [*parole*], 5, 18; *see also* discourse [*parole*]
Stalinism, 21, 29
Stirner, Max, 69, 101
Stoicism, 23
Strauss, Leo, 78
suicide, 85–6
surrealism, 63; *see also* Breton, André

technology, 31–3
  techno-democracy, 29, 31, 88
there is [*il y a*], 26–7
Thoreau, Henry David, 62, 92
Tocqueville, Alexis de, 30
Totalitarianism, 26, 29, 35, 38, 39, 40, 79, 80, 83, 95, 98, 99, 104, 107
  politics, relation to, 21–2
  techno-democratic totalitarianism, 29–31, 88
Tronti, Mario, 82–3
tyrannicide, 86

United States of America, 31, 70, 97–8
  university system, 103–4
universal extinction, 87–9
utopia, 4, 75–7
  'heterotopias', 76

Vaneigem, Raoul, 65
Vigny, Alfred de, 58

Wall Street, 3
Weil, Simone, 22, 56–7

Yakuza, 17

Žižek, Slavoj, 25

EU representative:
Easy Access System Europe
Mustamäe tee 50, 10621 Tallinn, Estonia
Gpsr.requests@easproject.com

www.ingramcontent.com/pod-product-compliance
Lightning Source LLC
Chambersburg PA
CBHW050244170426
43202CB00015B/2912